CUSTOMER SERVICE
INTERVIEW PREPARATION GUIDE

CUSTOMER SERVICE
JOB INTERVIEW GUIDE

CUSTOMER SERVICE
JOB INTERVIEW GUIDE

First Edition

ISBN 13:   978-1-9162991-4-6

Publisher's Note
Every possible effort has been made to ensure that the information contained in this book is accurate at the time of going to press, and the publishers and authors cannot accept responsibility for any errors or omissions, however caused. No responsibility for loss or damage occasioned to any person acting or refraining from action, as a result of the material in this publication can be accepted by the editor , the publisher or any of the authors.

British Library Cataloging-in-Publication Data
A CIP catalogue record for this book can be obtained from the British library

Printed in the United Kingdom
10 9 8 7 6 5 4 3 2

Contents

Contents

Attend

Conclude

Preface

The Learning Process

There are four phases to the learning process, as depicted by Abraham Maslow, these are as follows:

» Phase 1: Unconscious Incompetence
In this phase, we are unaware of our own incompetence

» Phase 2: Conscious Incompetence
In this second phase, we become aware of our incompetence

» Phase 3: Conscious Competence
In the third phase, we begin to understand and practice the correct way, but it takes a conscious effort

» Phase 4: Unconscious Competence
In the fourth and final phase, we can perform the new skill effectively without any conscious thought

Three Steps to Mastery

To successfully transition through conscious competence to unconscious competence, we must follow these three steps to mastery:

» Repeat
When we learn any new skill, we need to practice the skill many times until we can do it automatically. Studies suggest seven to twelve repetitions.

» Apply
When we are comfortable with our grasp of the new skill, we need to apply it to our daily life.

» Reinforce
When we have mastered the new skill, we need to keep it strong with continual use.

If you are willing to put a little time and effort into mastering the techniques in this book, you too will get the edge you need to pass the interview and live your dream - as many other readers have.

Quick Start Guide

Ideally you should allow one month or more to prepare. This will allow you ample time to study the material thoroughly, and apply the strategies without feeling too rushed.

However, it's not always the case that you will have this luxury of time. So, what's the best way to prepare when you only have a matter of weeks, or less?

Prepare your application materials (Page 55)
Whether or not your résumé is used to apply, you should get one drafted up as it will certainly assist you when filling in your application form. (Page 67)

Read what's relevant to your circumstances
If you struggle with any element in particular, maybe your confidence holds you back or you struggle to voice your opinion in group settings, put effort into developing those areas.

Gather facts about the company – (Page 14)
It would be a cardinal sin to arrive at the interview without having at least a basic knowledge of their operation, so do your research.

Prepare for potential questions – (Page 131-175)
At the very least, you should be prepared to answer questions such as:

- » Why do you want to become a (...)? (Page 167)
- » Why do you want to work for us? (Page 167)
- » Why should we hire you? (Page 168)
- » What are your weaknesses? (Page 170)

You should also be prepared with examples for competency based questions. (Page 131)

Rehearse
Rehearsing the interview process under simulated conditions will highlight potential areas of weakness. This will give you a better idea of where to focus your time and energy.

Prepare a list of questions - (Page 175)
Having intelligent questions prepared for the recruiters will set you apart as a prepared and enthusiastic candidate.

Prepare your outfit - (Page 45)
Presentation is the key to making a positive first impression, so prepare your outfit in advance.

Read what you can
The average reading speed is said to be 150-250 words per minute. This means that, even at the slower pace of 150 words, the whole book can be read in as little as a few hours. So, if you have just a few hours to spare after you have prepared, as per the above steps, make the most of this time allocation by reading as much as you can possibly comprehend.

Disclaimer

This book is designed to provide information and guidance on attending a customer service interview assessment. It is sold with the understanding that the publisher and author are not engaged in rendering legal or other professional services. Such topics, as discussed herein are, for example, or illustrative purposes only. If expert assistance is required, the services of a competent professional should be sought where you can explore the unique aspects of your situation and can receive specific advice tailored to your circumstances.

It is not the purpose of this guide to reprint all the information that is otherwise available to candidates but instead to complement, amplify and supplement other texts. You are urged to read all the available material, learn as much as possible about the role and interview techniques and tailor the information to your individual needs.

Every effort has been made to make this guide as complete and accurate as possible. However, this guide contains information that is current only up to the printing date. Interview processes are frequently updated and are often subject to differing interpretations. Therefore, there are no absolutes and this text should be used only as a general guide and not as the ultimate source of information.

All information in this book is offered as an opinion of the author and should be taken as such and used with discretion by the reader. You are solely responsible for your use of this book. Neither the publisher nor the author explicitly or implicitly promises that readers will find employment because of anything written or implied here.

The purpose of this guide is to educate and inform. The author and SpineBound Books shall have neither liability nor responsibility to you or anyone else because of any information contained in or left out of this book.

Prepare

Research

The Requirements

Person Specification

When making hiring decisions, employers consider three key elements, these are: eligibility, suitability and specific requirements. Together, these three elements form a 'person specification'. This person specification is referred to throughout the selection process to determine each candidates suitability for the position.

» Eligibility
Eligibility are the basic requirements which much be met in all circumstances. They are mostly based on facts and are likely to include level of education and previous experience.

Each company's eligibility criteria will be different to some degree so, to avoid disappointment, it is advisable to investigate each company's eligibility criteria before applying.

» Suitability
Unlike eligibility, which is based on facts, suitability is based on 'Core Competencies' and are determined by observation. Core competencies are a collection of personal qualities, skills, knowledge and experience that are necessary for optimal performance in the job.

There are several desirable characteristics for customer focused roles, such as being confident, friendly and calm, and there are four core competencies, these usually include team spirit, customer focus, communication competence and resilience

» Specific Requirements
Following the eligibility and suitability requirements, company's proceed to customise their requirements according to their specific standards and requirements.

These standards and requirements cover several criteria, and are subject to ongoing revision depending on the company's present requirements. For example:

Previous experience
A small company may view previous experience as a prime requisite while a prestigious and well established company may have no preference either way.

Specific skills and/or experience
If the company determines that there is a shortage of employees with specific skills and/or experience, a candidate possessing those may be valued more highly.

While performance is an obvious factor, the different and changing considerations which make up the person specification explain why it is possible to be rejected by one company but accepted by another, or unsuccessful on the first attempt and then successful at the next.

The Company

Selecting potential company's for which to apply is a fairly straightforward process and it is likely that you will have one or more company's already in mind. However, selecting a potential employer is an important decision which should be considered carefully and not taken lightly.

Before you jump in, you need to consider the following:

» The requirements
Do you meet the minimum requirements for the position? (See above)

» Location
Do you live within a reasonable travel distance? Would you be happy to travel this distance to and from every shift? or would you be happy to relocate?

» Salary & benefits
Are the salary and benefits sufficient to support your lifestyle?

» Corporate culture
'Corporate Culture' is a term used to describe the collective ideas, attitudes, beliefs, behaviours and values that exist within an organisation. In essence, it is the character of the airline.

Careful consideration of the corporate culture should be awarded because if there is a mismatch, it is unlikely that you will be happy working within that company in the long term.

Preliminary Research
Taking the time to research the company you want to work for will enable you to ask intelligent questions, as well as answer any that are posed. Your informed knowledge will give a positive impression about you and your motivation to work for the company, thus giving you a competitive edge over less informed candidates.

If you know nothing about the company other than the colour of the uniform and the salary, you certainly won't create a positive impression.

There is no need to know the whole history of the company, but you should at least know some basic information, such as:

» What are their staple products or services?

» Are there any future plans for expansion or growth?

» Who are the company's major competitors?

» What do you like about this particular company?

» How long have they been operating?

» Has the company won any awards? If so, which ones?

Note:

Read through some of the company's literature. Their website is a great place to locate this kind of information.

Journal Notes

Psychological Programming

> If you change the way you look at things, the things you look at change
>
> Dr. Wayne Dyer

Our performance is dictated by our psychology. If our minds are preoccupied with doubt, we certainly won't perform well and are unlikely to be successful through each stage of the selection process.

Successful candidates share similar attitudes and beliefs, and have learned to manage their state. The good news is that these success patterns can be learned and duplicated. The following pages contain tips and techniques that will enable you to program your mind for success.

Manage your Mind Set

Limiting beliefs are erroneous assumptions we hold about our own capabilities. They lurk in our subconscious mind and lead to self-sabotaging behaviours which prevent us from achieving our desired goals. These beliefs are mostly acquired subconsciously through outside influences and, once accepted and imprinted into our subconscious mind, will dictate how well we perform, interact and grow.

To move forward, these limiting beliefs must be identified and challenged, and then replaced with empowering beliefs.

Identify

Clearly it would be impossible to challenge or change a belief that we are unaware of, so the first step to transformation involves identification.

Some limiting beliefs are obvious and can be easily identified by their all or nothing words, such as 'always' or 'never', or 'can't' or 'impossible'. For instance:

- » My confidence always lets me down
- » There's too much competition, I can't compete
- » The interviews are impossible
- » I never say the right thing
- » I always fail

Some beliefs, however, are so deeply ingrained within our subconscious that we may not even be aware of their existence. To expose these, we can use a brainstorming session.

Brainstorming is a simple, yet powerful technique that produces raw material from the subconscious mind. To begin, simply sit down with a pad and pen and start writing down everything that comes to mind about the interview.

If you struggle for a place to begin, you could use the opening line "I want to pass the interview but..." then proceed to fill in the page until you run out of buts.

Asking relevant questions may also help, for instance:

» What meanings could I have created based on my past disappointments?

» What pessimistic thoughts reoccur every time I think about the interview?

» What unnecessary assumptions do I make about the interview?

» How might my standards be affecting my ability to relax?

» Am I holding onto any stereotypical beliefs that are holding me back?

Challenge

Now that we have identified our limiting beliefs, the next step is to challenge them. By challenging our old beliefs, we create doubt. This doubt is all we need to be able to slot a new empowering belief in its place. Strong beliefs are not always easy to destroy. These can, however, be weakened when they are challenged.

» Challenge the beliefs directly
The first way to break down a limiting belief is to question its validity. Challenge yourself to find evidence against it, and build a case that proves the assumption wrong. You could ask yourself questions, such as: How do I know this? Is it impossible or just hard? Is there another way I could look at this? Could there be another truth here?

» Question the source
Do you know where your assumptions came from in the first place? Did you choose these beliefs or are they by-products of someone else's belief systems? Sometimes, realising a belief is not ours is enough to destroy it.

» Challenge their usefulness
During our life, we have picked up beliefs that have not served us or were only valid for a certain period, but we have held onto them ever since. Ask yourself: Does this belief still serve a useful purpose? Does it help me move closer to my goals? Does this belief help or hurt me? If this belief limits me, how can I quickly get rid of it?

Note:

To gain the most benefit from the technique, you should write continuously for several minutes without stopping or judging, and without regard for spelling or grammar. When finished, re-read what you have written and circle any limiting beliefs.

> It's not the events of our lives that shape us, but our beliefs as to what those events mean.
>
> Anthony Robbins

» Weigh the consequences
The avoidance of pain is a great motivator, so realising the negative consequences of our beliefs, may provide the motivation we need to destroy it. Ask yourself: What has this belief cost me in the past? If I don't change this belief now, what will the consequences be in the future?

Replace
In this final step, we will identify and install alternative empowering beliefs. To do this, we simply need to reinforce each new belief with sufficient evidence to support it. Ask yourself: What have I done in my past that could contribute as evidence? What activities and actions could I take now that would strengthen this belief?

Keep a journal and continue creating evidence towards it. The more ingrained you can make the belief, the more evidence it will begin to identify for itself, and the deeper rooted the belief will become.

This step isn't an overnight process. It does take time to imprint the belief deeply enough into your subconscious that it will stick long term and overpower the old limiting belief but, with repetition and reinforcement, positive changes will begin to happen in your life.

Use your Imagination
Since our brain knows no difference between real or imagined experiences, it is possible to use mental rehearsal and visualisation techniques to manipulate our physiology and improve our interview performance.

Find a quiet space where you're unlikely to be disturbed for 10-15 minutes and use these basic guidelines:

» Get into a comfortable position and allow your body to relax. Take a few deep breaths and, as you exhale, imagine all of the tension slowly leaving your body.

Disassociate

If you struggle to visualise the experience from your own associated perspective, try observing yourself from a disassociated onlooker's perspective first.

» Now imagine it is the day of your interview and begin to visualise the entire day, scene by scene, in your subconscious. When running through the events in your mind, imagine feeling relaxed, yet energised as you converse effortlessly with other candidates and the recruiters. Observe how others warm to your friendly and confident nature. Imagine your composure as you intelligently answer the interviewer's questions.

» Make each scene as vivid and real as you can. Bring it closer, make the colours richer, sense the atmosphere in the room, and introduce sounds and feelings. Really intensify the experience.

» When you are pleased with the imagined performance, begin to introduce challenging scenarios for different characters you may encounter, questions you may be asked, and pressure you may be put under.

Using this rehearsal technique for just twenty minutes a day will train your brain to actually perform the new skills and behaviours.

Repetition is the key to success with this technique. The more you practice, the better you will get and the more confident you will feel.

Anchor your State

Anchoring is an NLP (Neuro Linguistic Programming) term which describes a process whereby certain psychological states, positive or negative, become associated with and can be triggered by a certain stimulus.

Using certain techniques, it is possible to anchor positive states so that we can readily access them on demand, or we can break the association of undesirable states using collapsing techniques.

Create an anchor

» Step 1: Identify
To begin the process of creating an anchor, we first need to identify the desirable state. For instance: confidence, calmness, assertiveness.

» Step 2: Locate a memory
Next we need to recall a particular time in our life when we have felt the desired state. The context is unimportant, but the experience must have been a powerful one.

» Step 3: Get into state
With an experience in mind, mentally put yourself back into that experience. Use all your senses to make the experience as vivid and intense as you can. What did you see? What could you hear? Where there any smells present? How did you look? How did you feel? Now really focus in and intensify those feelings.

» Step 4: Anchor the state
When the desired state has been captured and the feeling is about to hit its peak, it is time to anchor those feelings. This is done by firing off a unique combination of cues.

The cue combination can include one which is visual, one auditory, and one kinaesthetic. For example, pinching the skin above your knuckles, while visualising the colour blue, and saying the word 'YES' is a unique cue combination that would be appropriate.

Timing

The timing of your cues is critical. To be most effective, only fire up your cues at the very peak moment of the state, when it is most intense.

Uniqueness

The kinaesthetic cue you select should be unique. For example, scratching your palm, pinching the flesh above your knuckles and pulling the lobe of your ear are all unique gestures.

Repetition

Repetition really makes all the difference with this technique. The more you rehearse, the stronger you anchors will be.

Quick & Dirty Tip

To add bulk to a positive anchor, play videos that put you in positive states and fire your positive anchors during the peak state moments.

Important

The positive anchor must be stronger than the problem anchor. If the reverse is true, further reinforcement should be carried out to strengthen the positive anchor.

Stacking Anchors

The process of stacking anchors adds significant strength to anchors and simply involves eliciting several positive states into one set of cues.

» Step 5: Repeat
To really condition the anchor, repeat this procedure at least five times. The more repetitions, the stronger the anchor will be.

» Step 6: Test
Now that our anchor has been installed, we need to test its effectiveness. To do this, we simply need to fire off our unique cue combination that we set up in step 4.

For best results, break state for a few moments and think of something completely unrelated.

If the anchor has been a success, the desired state should be experienced within 10-15 seconds. If the feeling is not satisfactory, further reinforcement repetitions may be carried out, or the power of anchor stacking may be introduced.

Collapse an anchor

» Step 1: Identify
Before we begin the process of collapsing an anchor, we first need to identify the problem state (e.g. panic, anger, anxiety) and decide an alternative desired state that we would like to create in its place (e.g. confidence, calmness, assertiveness).

» Step 2 : Create
Next, we begin the process of creating anchors (See above). First we will create an anchor for the desirable state we want to capture. Then, we need to repeat the process for the undesirable state we want to collapse.

In creating these two anchors, we want to create the desirable anchor according to the steps outlined previously, however, the undesirable state should be created with less intensity in order to give the positive state more power.

This can be done effectively by simply visualising the negative state in less context, using fewer senses, and only using one kinaesthetic cue (be sure this cue is different to the one selected for the positive anchor)

» Step 3: Repeat
To really condition the anchors, repeat the procedure at least five times. The more repetitions, the stronger the anchor will be.

» Step 4: Test
Now that our anchors have been installed, we need to test their effectiveness. To do this, we simply need to fire off our unique cue combination.

For best results, break state for a few moments and think of something completely unrelated.

If the anchor has been a success, the state should be experienced within 10-15 seconds. If the feeling is not satisfactory, further reinforcement repetitions may be carried out, or the power of anchor stacking may be introduced.

» Step 5: Collapse
Finally, we begin the process of collapsing our problem anchor.

To do this, we simply fire both anchors at the same time. As you do this, your physiology will feel somewhat confused as it tries to achieve both states simultaneously. If the positive anchor has been created strong enough, the negative anchor will begin to clear. At this stage, we can let the negative anchor release, while we continue to fire and hold onto the positive state.

» Step 6: Test
To test the success of the collapse, break state for a few moments and try to re-fire the negative anchor. The result should be neutral. If the state persists the procedure may be repeated, using the power of stacking positive anchors.

Ask Resourceful Questions

When we ask questions of ourselves, we prompt our minds to search our internal memory archive for reasons and/or evidence to support those questions. So, whether we ask an empowering question, such as: "How can I achieve this?' or "Why am I so lucky?" or a disempowering question, such as: "Why does this always happen to me?" or "Why can't I ever get this right?" our brains will work to bring forth answers.

Wouldn't you rather have your brain bring back answers that create happiness and success? Well, why don't you make yourself a commitment to only ask empowering questions of yourself from this point forward? It's simple to do, and will really enhance the quality of your life.

Replace:

» "What's the point? I never pass anyway"

» "I always get nervous in interviews"

» "Why can't I be confident?"

With:

» "What steps can I take that will increase my chances of success?"

» "What can I do to manage my emotions?"

» "How can I feel confident right now?"

Re Frame your Words

Our confidence is shaped by our words. Changing the words we use can instantly change the way we think, feel and act.

For example, if we view the interview as a challenge and opportunity to grow, rather than a difficulty, our failures as feedback, and our mistakes as learning experiences, our whole physiology will become much more positive.

Similarly, when we say 'I can't', we are setting limitations on ourselves and will instantly cut ourself off from all possibility. Rather, we should try asking, 'how can I?' as this will challenge our brain to come up with solutions.

> I have not failed. I've just found 10,000 ways that won't work
>
> Thomas Edison

Adjust your Physiology

Our physiology has a direct impact on our psyche. Therefore, if we make some simple adjustments to our physiology, we can easily adjust our mood. To illustrate this point more clearly, try the following experiments:

Imagine for a moment that you harbour some self esteem issues and have a serious lack of confidence. Now ask yourself the following questions and then perform the appropriate corresponding movements:

If I were confident...

» How would I move?

» How would I sit?

» How would I sound?

» How would I look?

» How would I breathe?

» What gestures would I make?

Did you notice the change? Now try this:

» Curl your facial muscles up into a smile. Now, while maintaining this beautiful smile, try to become depressed or angry.

Now, anytime in the future that you find yourself in a negative state, use this technique to deliberately change it. If you feel unconfident, increase your confidence by acting like someone who has an abundance of it. If you feel sad, act like someone that is happy. If you feel tired, become energetic. If you feel angry... and so on.

Appear Confident

» Stand/sit tall with your shoulders back and head high
» Present a warm, relaxed smile
» Use open gestures
» Hold eye contact
» Breathe slowly and deeply
» Move with energy

Make the Swish

The swish pattern is a simple, yet very powerful sub modality technique which enables us to address unwanted and damaging behaviour responses, and replace them with appropriate and empowering ones. In essence, this method reprograms our brains neuro-associations.

For illustrative purposes, let's imagine that in stress provoking situations, such as an interview, we feel compelled to bite our nails. Clearly, this is an unwanted and unhelpful habit which does not create a positive impression. Using the swish method, we can completely and immediately eliminate this bad habit. Here's how we use the swish pattern:

Submodalities

Submodalities represent our five senses. I.e. Visual, auditory, kinaesthetic, olfactory and gustatory.

» Step 1: Identify the problem behaviour
First, we need to identify the problem behaviour. This could be one of many common problems such as: Stammering, blushing or trembling. Now, create an image that represents the habit or behaviour.

» Step 2: Identify the desired behaviour
Now identify an alternative behaviour and create a corresponding mental image of this state. For example: In the case of stammering, you may see yourself conversing clearly and effortlessly.

» Step 3: Identify suitable sub modalities
Identify and apply a sub modality that will reduce the desire for the problem behaviour in step 1 (E.g. Use a monochrome, unfocused image) and another that will increase desire for the empowering behaviour in step 2 (E.g. Increase the size, sounds and brightness).

» Step 4: Time to swish
Finally, we will use the swish pattern to replace the problem state. To do this, we will take the problem image from step 1, with the sub modality applied, and place it prominently in our mind.

Next we will take the desired image, also with the sub modality applied, and imagine it being placed into a sling shot. Now, imagine the sling shot drawing the image far into the distance, feel the tension of the elastic. Then, when ready to activate the swish, simply release the image from the sling shot and allow it to come hurtling forwards so that it smashes through the original image.

Allow the image to grow bigger, brighter, and more colourful. Let it completely fill your mind to make it really compelling.

To create even more power, we can include auditory and kinaesthetic cues to the pattern. For instance: we could say "whoosh" or "swish" while throwing a fist into the air.

» Step 5: Repeat
To reinforce the new behaviour, repeat step 4 at least 10 times in quick succession, each time making it faster. To avoid looping and reversing the pattern, it is important to break state between each cycle so that we always begin from and break through the starting image.

> Repetition of the same thought or physical action develops into a habit which, repeated frequently enough, becomes an automatic reflex
>
> Norman Vincent Peale

Find your Focus

What we focus on has a direct impact on how we feel and what we experience. So, when we focus on what we don't want, such as 'not feeling stressed' and 'not feeling unconfident' we only serve to attract more of these feelings because we are focusing all of our attention on them. Rather, we should focus on what we do want.

For instance:

Instead of:	Focus on:
Don't feel stressed	Feel calm and relaxed
Don't feel anxious	Feel alert and confident
Don't be upset	Feel joyful

Create Compelling Reasons

There may be challenging periods that arise during your interview which cause you to question your motives. If you have compelling reasons for wanting the job, your conviction will give you the driving force you need to carry you through these challenging moments.

So, ask yourself:

» Why do I really want this job?

» How will this job change my life?

» How will I feel when I am successful?

» What would I enjoy about the job?

Affirm & Incant

Affirmations and incantations are used to promote positive changes in our life.

Affirmations are short positive statements which are repeated several times in order to impress on our subconscious mind. To perform an affirmation, we simply take our chosen statement, for example "I am confident and successful in everything I do", and repeat it several times in quick succession with all the conviction and passion we can muster.

An incantation is a supercharged affirmation which also engages our physiology. This action of getting our body involved creates a much more powerful outcome.

> You become what you think about
>
> Earl Nightingale

Depending on how deeply ingrained our beliefs are, we may experience some strong resistance as our brain attempts to challenge the positive messages it is receiving. Thus, the effectiveness of both techniques relies on repetition, conviction and passion. The stronger your concentration, the deeper your faith and the more feeling you inject, the stronger the results will be and the faster changes will begin to occur.

The process of creating an affirmation involves a simple two step process:

» Step 1:
Think about areas in your life which you would like to improve and write them down. When you do this, focus on what you do want rather than what you don't want.

For example: I want to be confident
                 I want to be more assertive
                 I want to be liked
                 I want be calm

» Step 2:
Go through your list and write a positive affirmation   for   every desire. These may be in the present tense, such as: "I feel calm, confident and in control", or they may be releasing in nature, such as: "Every day I feeling calmer, more confident and in control". Your choice will depend on strength of resistance you experience. If there is only a slight feeling of resistance, continue with the present tense. If, however, the resistance is strong, you may start with a softer releasing statement until you begin to break through the barrier.

Sample present tense affirmations:

» "I experience love and joy with every part of my body"

» "I feel calm and am self disciplined"

» "I am a unique and special person"

» "I am beautiful because I am me"

» "I am respected and admired by others"

Sample releasing affirmations:

» "I am feeling happier and more self confident"

» "Every day I am feeling calmer and more disciplined"

» "I can feel my confidence growing stronger and stronger"

» "I love and appreciate myself more every day"

Supercharge

To supercharge your incantations further, try singing or chanting them.

Common Concerns

Unless there is some form of medical condition present, each of the common concerns listed below are generally symptoms of an underlying psychological element, such as anxiety. If these symptoms are psychologically driven, using the techniques described within this session will help manage, and even eliminate, these symptoms.

Challenge: Anxiety
Nervous feelings before an interview are quite legitimate and most people can relate to feeling tense or fearful on the run up to such an event. In fact, a little interview anxiety can make us more alert and really enhance our performance, so we would never want to completely eliminate interview anxiety. However, when that anxiety becomes strong enough to negatively affect our clarity of thought and dialogue, some anxiety management techniques should be introduced.

» Proper preparation
   Anxiety can be the result of poor preparation. If you anticipate potential questions, prepare appropriate answers, research the company and understand the requirements of the job, you will be better mentally prepared. If your mind is prepared, it makes sense that you will feel calmer, and more confident in yourself and your ability to handle the interview.

» Deep breathing
   Deep breathing will steady your rapid heartbeat, strengthen your shallow breathing, provide your brain with vital oxygen and make you more alert.

   Technique: Find a comfortable seating or standing position. Now, over the count of seven, inhale slowly and deeply through your nose. You should notice your stomach expand as your lungs begin to fill with oxygen.

   Now, over the count of 10-13 seconds, begin to exhale slowly through your mouth, allowing your stomach to gradually flatten. As you release the oxygen from your lungs allow your shoulders to relax and feel the tension release.

   Continue this pattern of in and out breaths until your breathing becomes steady and the anxiety subsides.

» Remediation
   Hypnotherapy, Cognitive Behavioural Therapy (CBT) and Neuro Linguistic Programming (NLP) sessions are very effective at dealing with deep rooted anxiety issues.

» Medication
If you find your anxiety levels quite literally overwhelm you at interviews, you may be considering medication. While this is a method I don't advocate, there are over the counter supplements, such as Kalms, St John's Wort, and Bachs Rescue Remedy, which can really help take the edge off anxiety. Otherwise, stronger prescription medications such as Xanex or Beta Blockers may be prescribed by your medical practitioner.

Challenge: Sweating

» Dress Colours
Black, navy and pure white will help disguise sweat marks, as will the camouflaging nature of patterns. Avoid: Light colours such as pale blue or grey.

» Dress Fabrics
Wear breathable fabrics such as: 100% cotton, pima cotton, seersucker, linen, 100% wool, merino, and cashmere. Avoid: Corduroy, flannel, silk, polyester and polyester blends, nylon, and acetate

» Dress Style
Wear loose fitting over and under garments for maximum air flow. Add layers, such as a suit jacket, waistcoat or cardigan, to disguise sweating.

» Antiperspirant
Use a clear, unperfumed antiperspirant. Beware: Antiperspirant can leave a film residue on your clothing. To avoid these stains, allow the antiperspirant to dry completely before putting on your shirt.

» Keep fresh
During bathroom breaks, wash your hands with lukewarm water. Blot your hands dry with a tissue and finish off with a light mist of a clear antiperspirant. Avoid: Cold or hot water, air dryers and sticky antiperspirants.

» Seek medical advice
Individuals with Hyperhidrosis, may seek the advice of a medical professional or dermatologist. Both can advise and prescribe suitable treatments, such as: Prescription strength antiperspirants and Botox.

Challenge: Not Enough Eye Contact
Good eye contact is one of the most important factors of body language. Shifty eyes, or complete avoidance of contact can suggest dishonesty, rudeness or lack of confidence. If you find eye contact anxiety provoking and uncomfortable, the following techniques will certainly help.

Warning

Always talk with your doctor before taking a medicine for the first time.

Challenge: Cotton mouth

» Keep fully hydrated by drinking plenty of water on the run up to the event. Fill up on water during breaks and periodically sip on water throughout the assessment.

» Stimulate saliva flow by adding a splash of lemon juice to your water bottle, sucking on sugar free candy or chewing sugarless gum. Gently biting your tongue can also activate the glands that stimulate saliva flow.

» Avoid salty and sugary foods, alcohol (including alcohol based mouthwash), caffeinated beverages and tobacco products as these inhibit saliva flow and dry the mouth out.

Note:

You should aim to maintain
eye contact 80 percent to 90
percent of the time.

» Use a mirror
Practice your eye contact by using your own mirrored image
as a guinea pig. When you see yourself in the mirror every day,
make a point of looking directly into your own eyes.

» Fake it
Rather than look directly into the eyes, you can fake it by either
directing your gaze at their eyebrows, forehead, or bridge of the
nose. This is not a permanent solution by any means, but it will
certainly ease you into the process.

» Avoid staring
In an attempt to forge eye contact, we may begin to stare. This
can indicate aggression and make others feel uncomfortable.
To avoid this extreme, lighten your gaze and keep it friendly. This
can be achieved by allowing your eyes to go slightly out of focus.

» Use opportunities
If you have notes, you can temporarily break eye contact as you
refer to these. Also, f there is a second recruitment officer present,
this will give you another opportunity to break eye contact as you
periodically direct your focus back and forth between the two.

Challenge: Blanking out
Even with all the preparation in the world, our mind can betray us
and draw a blank at the most inopportune moment. If this happens,
take a deep breath, remain composed and employ some of the
following techniques:

» Refer to your résumé
Your résumé provides an immediate memory jog in these
instances, so refer to it as and when necessary. You may also
want to jot down some key words or phrases inside a professional
looking notebook beforehand.

» Wait a moment
You don't have to always answer questions immediately. It is
perfectly permissible to pause and collect your thoughts before
proceeding with a response. In fact, taking the time to think
through your response can make you appear deliberate and
thoughtful. Answering without regard for your answer can make
you look impulsive.

» Be honest
If you don't have relative experience in a particular area, or
simply don't know the answer, you need to be honest and say so.
At this point, you could offer an alternative piece of information.

» Stall
If you feel you can get away with it, reflect the question back to
allow yourself a little more thinking time.

» Stay composed
Some recruiters will purposely throw in some curve ball questions to see how you react to pressure and think on your feet. In these cases, the interviewer is probably more interested in observing your reaction than they are about the answer you provide. So, stay calm and do your best to answer in a confident manner. In the worst case, simply be honest and admit you don't know the answer.

Challenge: Involuntary facial motions

Unless there is a medical condition present, involuntary facial twitching and trembling are generally ensuing of overly stressed muscles, such as forced smiling. These distressing symptoms are especially pronounced during an interview when we feel compelled to smile, or are attempting to conceal our nerves. To gain relief from these symptoms, we simply need to control how and when we smile.

Maintaining a constant grin is not only unnecessary and uncomfortable, it will also look insincere. Gentle and understated smiles are more than appropriate for prolonged periods, and full toothed smiles should be reserved for introductions and the occasional injection during conversation.

Next time you feel your facial muscles begin to tense, try relaxing your smile and see what a difference it makes.

Challenge: Fidgeting

Fidgeting, tapping and excessive gesturing with give the appearance of uncertainty, nervousness and unpreparedness. To effectively manage these movements, use the techniques outlined below.

» Identify
If you are unsure of any habits you may have, ask a friend, partner or coworker for their views. Alternatively, record yourself in a short mock interview and examine the footage. Mark down any ineffective mannerisms you can identify (playing with your pen, drumming your fingers, touching your face or hair, clearing your throat, or rubbing your nose) and then begin the process of eliminating each of them.

» Beware of props
Props can easily exaggerate any fidgeting, so if you have a pen, résumé or bag with you, avoid fiddling with them. Be equally mindful of jewellery, such as twirling earrings or a finger ring.

» Mind your hands
If the movements you employ are subtle, it is perfectly okay to gesture your arms and hands to endorse your words. Subtle means, keeping the movements below shoulder height and above the waist. If you find your movements become excessive or distracting, simply intertwine your fingers and rest your hands on the table or clasped loosely in your lap.

Challenge: Blushing

» Go green
A purposeful green pigmented concealer or foundation will minimise the impact of redness.

» Seek medical advice
Blushing which is caused by a medical condition should be treated by a medical professional. Prescription medication may be prescribed.

Challenge: Vocal paralysis

Under severe pressure, our voice may become partially paralysed. The physical symptoms of this may include stuttering, a weak and shaky vocal tone, or an unusually high pitch. These symptoms can be managed by adopting the following techniques:

» Speak in shorter phrases
» Slow your pace
» Control your breathing by using steady in-out breaths
» Maintain an upright posture
» Ignore the symptoms until they naturally relieve themselves
» Seek the assistance of a vocal coach

Gestures

Further information about gesturing and their usage can be found on page 35

Challenge: Perceived Arrogance

Sometimes, a high level of confidence may be misconstrued as arrogance. If you feel you are sometimes wrongly labelled as arrogant, the following guidelines will help you maintain your confidence, while avoiding this assumption.

» Be open
  We all have weaknesses, to say otherwise will certainly make you appear arrogant. Be clear about what you do and don't know, and be prepared to listen and learn from others.

» Be humble
  Act with humility when you are recognised for a job well done. Acknowledge the effort of others by sharing and giving praise where appropriate, and be accountable when errors transpire.

» Be approachable
  To make yourself appear more approachable, use open and inviting body language, and adopt a warm, friendly expression. Inject some personality into your conversations, make good use of eye contact (see above) and remember to use peoples names.

» Be considerate
  Genuinely acknowledge and compliment the hard work and efforts of others. Listen to and respect others opinions, and avoid interrupting when others are speaking.

Three Steps to Mastery

There are three basic steps to mastering the techniques introduced within this session, these are:

» Repeat
  When we learn any new skill, we need to practice the skill many times until we can do it automatically. Studies suggest seven to twelve repetitions.

» Apply
  When we are comfortable with our grasp of the new skill, we need to apply it to our daily life.

» Reinforce
  When we have mastered the new skill, we need to keep it strong with continual use.

> Use it or lose it
>
> Jimmy Connors

Put a little time and effort into mastering these techniques, and you will master any area of your life, even beyond the interview.

Journal Notes

Impression Management

Invent your Introduction

First impressions are absolutely critical for interview success. The impression you provide within the first few minutes will be the one that sticks and anything following will become merely a confirmation of that first impression. So, to assist you in getting off to the very best start, I have devised some tips that will help make you appear confident, friendly, relaxed and professional.

On arrival

Upon arriving at the venue, approach the reception desk and introduce yourself, your purpose and whom you are expecting to meet. For example:

> "Hello. My name is Jane Doe and I'm here for an interview with Carrie Loren"

Once signed in, thank the receptionist and take a seat in the waiting area.

Meeting the candidates

If you are attending an open day or group selection process where other candidates will be present, you will have many introductions to contend with. These introductions are just as important as any other and must not be underestimated.

Candidate introductions should be handled in much the same way as any other, however, you may keep these slightly less formal if you wish. As you approach the candidate(s), smile and make eye contact, then say hello and introduce yourself. In a one to one introduction, offer a handshake if you so desire. In a group introduction, a handshake is unnecessary. If the candidate(s) responds positively to your approach, you may engage in further small talk.

Meeting the recruiter(s)

When you meet each recruiter for the first time, be sure to stand up straight, make eye contact and smile. Then, allow the recruiter to initiate the introduction and the handshake.

> » If they greet you by name, your response should be:
> "Hello Ms. Loren. It's a pleasure to meet you".

> » If an introduction is needed, simply say:
> "I'm Jane Doe. It's a pleasure to meet you" or
> "Hello Ms. Loren. Pleased to meet you. I'm Jane Doe"

At this stage, pleasantries may be initiated by the recruiter as a way to break the ice. Just follow their lead and go with the flow.

Warning

Take great care with candidate introductions, and read their body language on approach. Some candidates may be stand-offish because they see you as competition, while others may need some alone time with their thoughts. If you feel any sense of displeasure from your approach, back off immediately.

Consider your Communication

Because effective communication skills are essential for interview success, it is important to be mindful of how our communication is received. This means that we must consider not only the words we use, but also how our tonality and body language complement or contradict those words.

Consider the following communication guidelines:

Word Choice

Words are important because they communicate and convey our message succinctly. So, even at a low 7% accountability, our word choice can mean the difference between a powerful, captivating and influential exchange, and a weak, disempowering and ineffective one. To create the desired response, consider the following guidelines:

» Action Words
  Action words are positive, powerful and directive, and should be used abundantly. Action words include: Communicated, conveyed, directed, listened, persuaded, arranged, handled and improved. **A complete list of action verbs can be found on page 101**

» Filler Words
  Anyways, you know how when you are, like, really nervous, and you ,ummm, find it hard to verbalise and stuff, and you say silly things that, kind of, make you sound, like, kind of, unprofessional and maybe, like, inarticulate?

  The useless and annoying verbal mannerisms used in the above example "you know," "like," "in other words," "kind of," "ummm," and "anyways." should be avoided at all costs. Besides sounding unprofessional, they also distract attention from the message.

» Undermining Words
  Words and phrases such as 'I think,' 'I hope,' 'maybe,' 'sort of,' 'perhaps,' 'I guess,' all undermine your message and credibility by creating the impression that you don't trust your own knowledge or opinion. Eliminating these phrases will drastically improve the quality of any message.

» Jargon, Slang and Clichés
  Specialist terminology and informal expressions can confuse an outside audience. Avoid these where possible, and stick to simple, clear and coherent language.

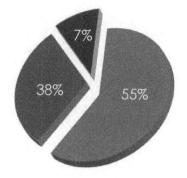

7% Words

38% Tonality

55% Body Language

The 1971 study, conducted by Albert Mehrabian, suggests that our words account for only 7% of our overall communication, while tonality accounts for a further 38% and body language accounts for a massive 55%.

Tonality

Our tonality plays a key role in sending the correct messages. So, if our aim is to project confidence, enthusiasm and expertise, it is important to exercise control and awareness of our tonality throughout our interactions.

» Pitch

Pitch refers to the degree of highness and lowness in our voice. A variation in our pitch creates meaning, adds clarity and makes what we are saying more interesting. For instance: A rise in our pitch suggests we are asking a question, which indicates doubt, uncertainty and hesitation. A fall in pitch indicates a statement, which further suggests certainty and assurance.

» Tempo

Tempo refers to the speed of our voice. If we speak too slowly, we risk losing the interest and attention of our audience. If we speak too fast, others may find us difficult to follow. The key is to maintain a pace which is fast enough to maintain interest, yet slow enough to be clear.

» Volume

Volume refers to the loudness of our voice. Speaking in a loud volume suggests aggression, while a quiet volume indicates shyness and makes it difficult to be heard. The key to determining the appropriate volume is to keep your voice loud enough to be heard, but soft enough to be clear. Modulation of volume can also be introduced to keep the speech interesting and add extra emphasis.

» Articulation

Articulation refers to our vocal clarity. Regardless of our pitch, tempo, volume and accent, we need to make a conscious effort to enunciate clearly.

Body Language

The way we carry ourselves, the gestures we use and our facial expressions communicate all sorts of messages, so learning to control certain aspects of these can help us to convey the message of a well-balanced, confident individual.

» Gestures

We use open gestures when we are feeling confident and relaxed, and are being honest and sincere. Therefore, to be perceived as relaxed, sincere and confident, keep your arms unfolded, your legs uncrossed and your palms open.

Recommended:

For those of you interested in voice training, I highly recommend a program by Roger Love called 'The Perfect Voice'.

Further information about this program can be found at www.rogerlove.com

Caution

Because gestures are culture specific, it is important to exercise caution when around people from other cultures.

Different meanings may be unintentionally conveyed, and can easily lead to confusion and misunderstanding.

Gesturing can also be useful for adding emphasis to what we are saying and, if the movements we employ are subtle and controlled, it is perfectly okay to use gestures to express ourselves and endorse our words. For best results, keep any movements below shoulder level, but above the waistline.

If you find your movements become excessive or distracting, simply rest your hands on the table or loosely in your lap.

Open Palms
Open palms signify honesty and give the impression of a relaxed and confident person.

Steepling fingers
This gesture is understood to be a sign of confidence and authority.

Nodding your head in agreement when the recruiter is speaking will signal that you are listening and understand. However, be careful not to over emphasise the movement.

» Movement
The way we carry ourselves is a powerful indicator of how we feel. To be perceived as confident and professional, walk briskly with an erect posture. Keep your shoulders back, your arms loosely at your side, and chin parallel to the floor.

» Posture
To portray the image of a confident and motivated person, adopt an upright and attentive posture that is open, yet relaxed. Keep your chin parallel to the floor, shoulders back and spine straight.

If seated, lean slightly forward with your hands loosely in your lap, or on the table. Place both feet flat on the floor, or cross your ankles.

If standing, keep your arms loosely at your side or behind your back and plant your feet about 8-10 inches apart. If standing for long periods, place one foot slightly in front of the other to allow you to smoothly and unnoticeably shift weight between your feet.

Top Ten Negative Gestures

» Finger Pointing
» Fist Pounding
» Karate Chopping
» Finger Drumming
» Hand Wringing
» Oversized Gestures
» Feet Tapping
» Arm Crossing
» Pen Clicking
» Hair Twirling

Tip

To achieve good posture, stand with your back to the wall and look straight ahead. In this position, your head, shoulders and bottom should touch the wall.

Avoid

» The John Wayne:
Feet wide apart with hands on hips.
» The fig leaf:
Feet close together with hands crossed over genital area.

Both stances will guarantee you a loss of respect and power instantly.

» Facial Expressions
Our facial expressions convey a wide range of attitudes, feelings and emotions, and these can have a significant impact on our ability to connect with others. Because of this, it is important to be aware of the story our face is telling and work to convey an attentive, sincere and interested expression.

A positive expression can certainly include a smile, but doesn't necessarily imply its inclusion. In fact, maintaining a constant smile is not only uncomfortable, it is also completely unnecessary. Instead, an open expression that includes a gentle and understated smile, soft eyes and slightly elevated eyebrows will result in a soft and pleasant expression.

Large smiles should be reserved for introductions and the occasional injection during conversation.

Tip:

If you hands are naturally sweaty, try using unscented antiperspirant on your hands.

» Handshake
Your hand shake says a lot about you. A firm handshake conveys confidence, assertiveness and professionalism. A weak, limp handshake suggests shyness and insecurity, and a strong, crushing handshake indicates aggression and dominance.

To perform a professional and confident handshake, follow these simple guidelines:

Before connecting for the handshake establish eye contact, smile and lean slightly forward. As you extend your right hand, keep your hand straight and thumb pointing upwards. When your hands connect engage a firm, but not crushing, grip. Shake one to three times, for a duration of 1-3 seconds, and break away.

» Eye Contact
Good eye contact is one of the most important factors of body language. Shifty eyes, or complete avoidance of contact can suggest dishonesty, boredom, rudeness, insecurity or shyness.

Note:

You should aim to maintain eye contact 80 percent to 90 percent of the time.

If you find eye contact anxiety provoking and uncomfortable, direct your gaze at their eyebrows, forehead, or bridge of the nose. This is not a permanent solution by any means, but it will certainly ease you into the process.

In an attempt to forge eye contact, be aware not to stare as this can indicate aggression and make others feel uncomfortable. To avoid this extreme, lighten your gaze and keep it friendly. This can be achieved by allowing your eyes to go slightly out of focus.

If you have notes, you can temporarily break eye contact as you refer to these. Also, f there is a second recruitment officer present, this will give you another opportunity to break eye contact as you periodically direct your focus back and forth between the two.

» Eye Cues

As with our facial expressions, our eyes reveal much about how we are feeling. This could be through our eye contact, blink rate, or eye movements.

We blink, on average, 10 times per minute. When we are relaxed, our blink rate reflects this slower rate. When we are anxious, uncomfortable or being dishonest, our blink rate increases.

Our eye movements, eye accessing cues, reveal whether we are accessing a memory, or constructing one. While it is debated as to whether we can catch someone lying by watching their eye direction, we can certainly determine what sensory system they are accessing.

VC - Visual Constructed

This would be the direction a persons eyes moved in when they are constructing new visual images.

AC - Auditory Constructed

This would be the direction a persons eyes moved in when they 'auditorily construct' a sound in their mind.

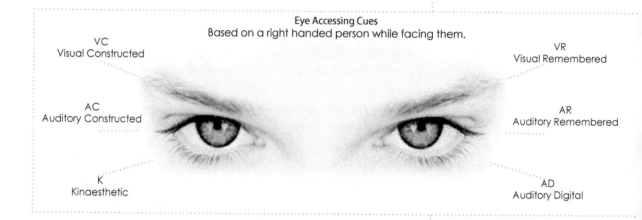

Eye Accessing Cues
Based on a right handed person while facing them.

VC
Visual Constructed

AC
Auditory Constructed

K
Kinaesthetic

VR
Visual Remembered

AR
Auditory Remembered

AD
Auditory Digital

AR - Auditory Remembered

This would be the direction a persons eyes moved in when they are remembering sounds from the past.

AD - Auditory Digital

This would be the direction a persons eyes moved in when they access internal dialogue

K - Kinaesthetic

This would be the direction a persons eyes move in as they recall a smell, feeling or taste.

VR - Visual Remembered

This would be the direction a persons eyes moved in when they are visually remembering the past.

Communication Barriers

Barriers to effective communication may arise for a number of reasons. When these barriers do occur, we are forced to become even more effective in our ability to communicate. The strategies below will help overcome some of these more effectively.

» Language
Language barriers can be a challenge if you are interviewing with an international organisation or have a very strong accent. In either case, speak slowly and clearly, ask for clarification and check for understanding, avoid idioms and jargon, use gestures and be specific, listen actively and be patient.

» Gender
Barriers in communication between genders exist primarily because men and women have different communication patterns. To overcome these barriers, it is important to appreciate, learn and understand the different strengths and styles that exist.

While men tend to be more direct and factual, women tend to be indirect and tactful. Men have a preference for reason and logic, are competitive and are interested in power, rank and status. Women are empathetic and feeling oriented. They value relationships and like to build rapport. Men communicate to exchange information and solve problems, while women communicate to share and a build connection.

» Emotional
Emotional barriers within an interview situation manifest themselves through fear, shyness or restraint. When we feel distracted by these emotional states, our ability to communicate at an effective level is severely inhibited. We may wrongly interpret the actions and words of others, and may not effectively express our own opinion. We may even stop listening to the other person as our internal dialogue takes over.

To effectively deal with these barriers, it is important to treat the underlying cause of such emotions. This can be achieved with psychological intervention (see pages 17-25).

Create a Connection

To form a memorable impression and influence the recruiters hiring decision in our favour, it is important to make an effort to connect. Mirroring is a very effective connecting strategy because of its ability to create rapport and trust.

As the name suggests, mirroring is a process whereby our communication style and body language mirror those of the recruiter. Providing our imitations are subtle and not obvious in any way, adapting our speaking style and movements can help the recruiter relate with us and feel more comfortable.

Communication Style

Mirroring communication style can be done through using similar words or phrases, matching the sensory style, or mimicking the pitch, tempo and volume of their voice.

» Words and Phrases
We can make a fantastic psychological impact simply by injecting the recruiters own terminology and sequence of words into our answers. For example, if the interviewer points out that they are looking for and value a candidate who is 'team spirited, customer focused and efficient', simply stating that we are 'good with customers, work well in a team and always make an effort', while implying the same values, will not create the same strong psychological impact.

» Pitch, Tempo and Volume
Matching our pitch, tempo and volume to the recruiters speaking style will make us appear in tune to what they are saying. This will speed up the rapport process and greatly improve our chances of creating a favourable impression.

» Sensory Style
While we all use a mix of the sensory styles: Visual, kinaesthetic and auditory, we tend to have a dominant style that we gravitate towards. If, during the course of the interview, it becomes obvious that the recruiter has a preference towards a particular sensory style, you can adjust your style accordingly to establish a deeper connection.

Visual people prefer to see how things are done rather than just talk about them. They are neat and orderly and take pride in their appearance. They speak rather quickly and use words that reflect their visual style, such as: 'I see what you mean', 'It looks to me like...', 'I imagine that...'

Auditory people like to use their voice and can easily go into lengthy discussions. They enjoy reading aloud and will often talk to themselves while working. Their style can be identified by their medium pace of speech and use of hearing words, such as: 'I hear what you are saying', 'We'll discuss this further', 'I hear you loud and clear'

Kinaesthetic people are very physically orientated and like to move a lot. They have difficultly sitting for long periods and use lots of expressive gestures as they speak. Their style can be identified by their slow pace and use of action words, such as: 'It feels as if...', 'It slipped my mind', 'I have a solid grasp...'

Movements

» Matching and mirroring
When people have a strong connection with one another, they will subconsciously copy each other's body language. To quickly create a strong connection with the recruiter, the same technique may be applied.

As you are speaking with the recruiter, make a mental note of how they are sitting and what they are doing with their hands. Then, subtly mirror their position and gestures. If they are leaning forward, you might lean forward also. If they have their hands clasped on the table, you might do the same.

The key to successfully utilising this technique is subtlety. If we become obvious by reacting instantly to each and every change, the effectiveness of the technique will be lost. Similarly, if we mirror closed signals, we may accomplish only a negative connection.

The best time to mirror a position is when we engage in dialogue. For example: The recruiter leans forward as they begin to ask a question. As we engage our follow up response, a change in position would appear natural and go completely unnoticed.

» Leading
Leading is an influencing technique which can be used to judge the level of connection. For example: If you feel you have achieved rapport with the recruiter and both of you have your hands in your lap and are sat up straight, you could lean forward slightly and clasp your hands gently onto the table. If the recruiter follows your lead, you can be sure that you have established a strong connection.

Disconnection

It is important to be perceptive to signs that the recruiter has become disconnected so that we can be proactive in re-establishing a connection.

Before attempting to reconnect, however, it is important to establish the accuracy of our perceptions because we may have simply misread the signal or it could be a by-product of our paranoid imagination. Similarly, the perceived signal may be a momentary motion that has no substance or it may be unrelated to us entirely.

To reliably determine the accuracy of our observation, we first need to scan for clusters of signals that are supportive of our perception. If we observe two or more congruent signals, this is a definite cluster. Next, we can test our connection by attempting to 'lead' (see above). If the recruiter doesn't follow, this is also a sure sign that a disconnection has taken place.

Master the Art of Small Talk

Recruiters recognise that job interviews are nerve wracking events and will usually open the session with a brief period of small talk. Perhaps this is an attempt to merely break the ice, or possibly a way to judge your communication and people skills while under pressure. Either way, your involvement can have a direct impact on your overall success and consideration for your responses should be given.

To help you successfully navigate your way through the minefield of interview small talk, I have prepared the following guidelines.

» Stick to safe topics
  Keep your focus on positive or neutral topics such as the weather and traffic. Discussions about politics or religion should be avoided, as should negative or controversial current events. Each of these can stir up some very strong emotions and shift the interview in a negative direction very quickly.

» Show interest
  While discussions about the weather and traffic are not particularly engaging, an effort should be made to look interested.

» Give short responses
  Small talk should remain small. Long winded stories about the journey, the weather, or the latest sports news are not only unnecessary, they are also inappropriate. Respond in a conversational tone, but don't get carried away.

» Be sincere
  Being friendly too quickly or being overly complimentary may appear desperate and insincere. To be effective, keep pleasantries minimal and sincere.

Disconnection Signals

Signs of disconnection include:
» Fake smile
» Yawning
» Closed gestures
» Stretching
» Using barriers
» Shifting
» Directing their body away
» Tidying the desk
» Writing notes
» Slouching
» Fidgeting

Disapproval Signals

Signs of disapproval include:
» Pursed lips
» Frowning
» Eye squinting
» Jaw clenching
» Increased blinking rate
» Shaking head
» Licking lips
» Scratching
» Rubbing eyes

» Be positive
There is no room for negativity of any kind. Even if you had trouble finding the location or got stuck in a long traffic jam on your way to the venue, a positive response is the only one that should be considered. For instance:

"How was your journey?"
"Very good, thank you"

"I hope the traffic wasn't too terrible?"
"I expected a little traffic, so I left early for this reason"

"Did you find the venue okay?"
"Yes, thank you. I found your map to be a great help"

» Control your body language
Even during this seemingly informal discussion, our body language is important. Convey a professional and confident message by maintaining steady eye contact, keeping an upright posture and wearing a warm smile.

Plan an Exit Strategy

When the interview approaches its conclusion, regardless of what has happened and how we feel, it is important to depart gracefully for that final lasting impression.

Tip:

If a panel of recruiters are present, a handshake for each person is unnecessary. Simply thank the panel and shake hands with whomever escorts you to the door.

Note:

If the recruiter initiates a handshake, be sure to rise to a full standing position before taking their hand.

» Step 1: Gather your belongings
Before rising, gather your belongings and ensure a firm grip. If possible, leave your right hand free for the inevitable final handshake.

» Step 2: Straighten your clothing
As you rise from your seat, be sure to straighten up any disjointed attire such as your tie, jacket or skirt.

» Step 3: Exchange pleasantries
Once standing, smile and say "Thank you for taking the time to meet with me today". Then, if expected, exchange handshakes and make your way to the door.

» Step 4: Make your exit
Stop at the door, turn, smile and say a final "thank you". Then proceed with your exit and be sure to close the door behind you.

Journal Notes

Polish your Image

During the first few minutes of the interview, the recruitement team will make certain judgements about a candidates character and suitability based on their appearance. Thus, if we are to succeed in creating that all important positive first impression, it is essential that we make a valid effort to present a polished and conservative image.

To help you achieve this, I have prepared the following guidelines.

Organise your Outfit

Business casual may be perfectly acceptable for some companies and it is the very least that should be considered. An acceptable minimum standard for casual business wear for women is no less than a reasonable length dress skirt or tailored trousers with a blouse or cardigan/sweater combination. For men, a collared shirt and trouser combination would apply.

For maximum impact, however, classic formal business attire is a safe choice that will give a clean, polished and professional appearance.

Whatever style of dress you ultimately choose, whether formal or informal, you need to pay attention to:

» Fit:
  Wear clothing that fits your body correctly. Clothing that is too short or too long, too big or too small is never a good look.

» Suitability:
  Even if you opt for a casual look, your attire needs to be suitable. Too much cleavage, exposed midriffs, and excessively short skirts are not suitable, so don't do it.

» Patterns:
  Some patterns can appear overwhelming, so play it safe with a solid colour or stick to conservative and subtle patterns such as pinstripes.

» Colours:
  Too much colour can also be overwhelming, so wear traditional colours, such as: navy blue, charcoal grey and black, and introduce colour sparingly and subtly through your shirt/blouse or tie. This will give your outfit a professional, yet unique character.

» Fabric:
  Some fabrics wrinkle easily, so look for a suit that is made of a wrinkle resistant fabric such as wool.

Gents

Tie

» Select a tie colour that is conservative and a pattern that is subtle. Exuberant patterns or character ties should be avoided.

» For a strong and confident look opt for a larger knot, such as the Pratt or Windsor.

» The optimum length of a tie is one which falls to the same level as the belt buckle.

» Tie bars and clips may be worn to keep the tie in place.

Pratt Tie Knot

Double Windsor

Shirt

» Choose a good quality 100% cotton shirt which has long sleeves.

» Subtle patterns are generally acceptable, but avoid horizontal stripes.

» Select a colour which compliments your suit and contrasts your tie. White and blue are the most conservative choices.

» Cuff link style cuffs are fine, as are buttoned down styles.

Suit Style

» A well tailored suit in a wrinkle free fabric will create a sophisticated and professional image.

» Traditional colours, such as navy blue, black and charcoal grey are the most formal and professional.

» Solid colours or subtle patterns are acceptable choices.

» A matching jacket will create a professional and neat look, and build credibility.

» A well fitting suit jacket is one which buttons up easily, without a significant tug across the fabric, and where the shirt cuffs extend a 1/4 of an inch beyond the jacket cuffs when relaxed.

Belt

Your belt must feature a conservative buckle and the strap should coordinate with the colour of your shoes.

Socks

Socks should be dark and long enough to cover skin when seated. Mid-calf length is ideal for this purpose.

Shoes

Shoes should be clean and neat and in a style and colour which complements the overall look of the outfit.

Ladies

Blouse

» Choose a good quality and conservative blouse which has shoulders and sleeves.

» Avoid low cut necklines and button up at least two buttons up from the cleavage line.

» Subtle patterns are generally acceptable, but avoid horizontal stripes.

» Select a colour which compliments your suit. White and off white are the most conservative choices.

Suit Style

» A well tailored suit in a wrinkle free fabric will create a sophisticated and professional image.

» Traditional colours, such as navy blue, black and charcoal grey are the most formal and professional.

» Solid colours or subtle patterns are acceptable choices.

» A matching jacket will create a professional and neat look, and build credibility.

Skirt, Dress or Trousers

Skirts and dresses provide a more streamlined and feminine appearance, however, a trouser suit is an acceptable choice so you should proceed with your personal preference.

Skirts and dresses must be a conservative length that is no less than knee length.

Always opt for loose fit trousers, rather than tight fit.

Shoes

Shoes should be clean and neat and in a style which complements the overall look of the outfit.

Closed court shoes in a low to medium heel are safe choices.

Hosiery

For a sophisticated look, tights or stockings in a natural colour should be worn.

Tend to your Grooming

» Hands & Nails
Ensure that your nails are clean, neatly trimmed and reasonable in length. Nail polish should be conservative and match in colour. Avoid charms, glitter and multicoloured polish.

» Cosmetics
Use cosmetics to conceal blemishes and enhance your assets but avoid going over the top. Less is more in a formal interview setting where a natural and polished look will be appreciated.

» Hair
Hair should be neat and well groomed, and outrageous colours or styles should be avoided. Frizzy or loose ends can appear messy so should be brushed into place and fixed, but be careful not to produce a slicked down appearance.

Accessorize

» Perfume & Cologne
If you choose to wear perfume or cologne, select a light scent and wear it sparingly.

» Jewellery
Keep jewellery minimal and conservative. Wear no more than one ring per hand and avoid oversized pieces.

» Watch
Wear a simple working watch which doesn't beep.

» Portfolio
Consider carrying a small leather portfolio rather than a briefcase or everyday handbag. Portfolios are simple, organised and easy to carry.

» Tattoos & Facial Piercings
Visible tattoos and facial piercings are not ideal. For peace of mind, conceal visible tattoos and remove facial piercings.

The Final Countdown

The Run Up

» Rehearse
On the final run up to the event, set aside some time to go through a final rehearsal of your presentation. Practice answering questions and going over talking points with a friend or relative and use this opportunity to iron out any wrinkles.

» Perform a dry run
If possible, take the opportunity to visit the venue in advance. This dry run will familiarise you with the route, parking and travel time and allow you to avoid becoming lost or late on the day. If you can do the route at the same time of day, you'll benefit from the added simulation of traffic and road conditions.

If you are unable to make an advance visit the venue, use the internet to map out a detailed route map that also provides distance and time estimations.

» Inspect your outfit
A few days before the event, take out the outfit you plan to wear and make sure it is clean, pressed, and has no buttons missing. Have it dry cleaned and repaired if necessary.

» Get a hair cut
Consider having your hair cut a week out from the day. This will allow the cut to soften slightly for a more natural look, while still retaining some of the freshness of the cut.

» Calm your nerves
If you feel your anxiety levels begin to escalate, put aside time to practice the strategies outlined on pages 17 through 31.

The Evening Before

» Review your résumé
As you complete a final review of your résumé, notice and take pride in your listed achievements. Take the time to remind yourself of why you want the job and what you have to offer.

» Check travel arrangements
If travelling by car, make sure the tank has plenty of petrol and that you have change available for parking meters. If using public transport, check timetables.

To keep your vocal cords sufficiently lubricated, you must keep hydrated.

Make sure you drink plenty of water 24 hours before the event.

Three litres of water per day is the ideal volume.

» Prepare your outfit
Take out the outfit you plan to wear and go through a final inspection to make sure it is clean and pressed. Inspect your hosiery for runs or holes. Clean and polish your shoes. Prepare your accessories and gather your portfolio pieces. Then, lay the pieces out ready for the morning.

» Organise your portfolio
To avoid a morning rush, prepare your portfolio in advance.

» Get an early night
To ensure you are fresh and alert, you'll need a good night's sleep. So, aim to retire no later than 11 pm. A warm aromatherapy bath before bed will help you relax and unwind.

» Set your alarm
Before winding down for the night, ensure your alarm is set to the appropriate time. For caution, you may set two alarms or enlist a relative to give you a friendly wake up call.

On the Day

» Drink a glass of water
As soon as you rise, rehydrate and wake up your system with a large glass of water.

» Stretch
Incorporating a full body stretch into your morning routine will increase blood flow and wake up your tired muscles.

» Psyche yourself up
Jump start your motivation by chanting your incantations, acknowledging your goals and visualising your success.

» Listen to music
Listening to your favourite upbeat music is a great way to put you in a good mood. It will lighten the atmosphere and increase your energy level.

» Eat a good breakfast
Oatmeal is light, natural and slow releasing so it will provide ample energy for the day. Perhaps combine it with a protein shake and piece of fruit for a power breakfast.

» Leave with plenty of time to spare
Arriving late to an interview means you immediately start the interview from behind the rest of the candidates. You also risk arriving in a panic. You should, therefore, aim to arrive at least 15 minutes early and allow extra travelling time to account for any unforeseen delays.

It is better to be an hour early than it is to be just a minute late. You can always grab a coffee and go through your notes.

Portfolio Essentials

Documentation
» Copies of your résumé
» Interview invitation
» A copy of your application form
» Certificates
» Reference details.

A notepad
A notepad is tidier than lots of pieces of paper.

2 pens
With two pens, you will have a backup if the first runs out of ink or becomes lost. Alternatively, you can lend one to another candidate.

A pencil and eraser
These two items are a must as they will make any mistakes easy to rectify.

Smokers Beware!

Stale smoke will linger on your clothing for hours, so avoid smoking before or during the interview.

On Arrival

» Freshen up
  If you have time, and it's convenient to do so, take a moment when you arrive to freshen up. Inspect your outfit, wash your hands, touch up your makeup, pop in a breath mint and spritz some deodorant. Be sure to discard any gum or breath mints before you enter to announce your arrival.

» Turn off your cell phone
  To avoid potential interruptions, turn off your cell phone or put it on silent mode as soon as you arrive.

Journal Notes

Journal Notes

Apply

Introduction

There are several ways you can register your interest for a position, these include:

» Traditional paper cover letter and résumé/application form combination

» Email cover letter with digital résumé/application form

» Online application facility

In recent years, many companies have moved onto, and prefer, online application facilities. As a result, it would be wise to check with each company before proceeding with any of the alternative methods. If, however, you don't have easy access to the internet it is generally acceptable to request a postal application pack or submit your résumé to the company's recruitment office for consideration.

Whichever method you ultimately select, the following pages contain detailed guidance notes that will assist you with each format.

So, without further ado, let's proceed with this important section on applying...

Write a Winning Cover Letter

Font Comparisons

Serif Fonts

Font	Size
Arial	14
Arial	12
Arial	11
Arial	10
Verdana	14
Verdana	12
Verdana	11
Verdana	10

Sans Serif Fonts

Font	Size
Georgia	14
Georgia	12
Georgia	11
Georgia	10
Garamond	14
Garamond	12
Garamond	11
Garamond	10

SansSerif

Serif

A cover letter is a valuable opportunity to introduce yourself and highlight your suitability for the role. Use the guidelines below to ensure a strong first impression.

Appearance

» Paper
Keep to the standard paper size of your geographic location. In Europe, this is 210x297mm and in the United States, it is 8.5x11".

A quality uncoated paper, such as bond, linen and laid, is often used for corporate stationery and, as such, can give your letter an important feel. Don't be overly concerned with this aspect, though, as its significance is minimal.

» Decoration
Avoid decoration such as floral borders or marble background effects. Instead, add some character by using a personalised logo.

» Length
One page is ideal. Any longer, and you risk losing the reader's interest

» Margins
Use acceptable business format margins of .75" to 1.0" left and right

» Spacing & Alignment
Your letter should be single spaced, flush left, with each paragraph separated by a blank line.

» Fonts
Use a popular font that is clear, easy to read and not overly decorative. Universal fonts such as Georgia, Arial and Verdana work well.

Use an adequate font size that is large enough that the reader doesn't have to squint, no less than 9 or 10 points, but not so large that the letter doesn't fit on the page, around 12 points.

Conventions

Addresses

- » Return Address
  Europe: Top centre or right-hand corner
  America: Top left-hand corner

- » Recipients Address
  In Europe, the recipients address is placed at the left side of the page. Either on the same line as, or one line below, the date line. In America, it is placed two lines below the return address at the left side.

```
Mr / Mrs / Ms / Miss ...
Company
Building Number, Street
Address Line 2
City
State/County
Zip/Post Code
COUNTRY (in capital letters)
```

Date

- » European format: 15 May 2008
  Positioned on the right, one line below the return address.

- » American format: May 15, 2008
  Positioned at the top left-hand corner, above the return address.

Opening Salutation
A more favourable impression will be created if you make an effort to find out the name of the person who is accepting applications and then address him/her personally.

Use the title (Mr, Mrs, Miss or Ms) followed by the, correctly spelled, surname

- » Dear Ms Loren

If, despite your best efforts, you cannot obtain the addressees name, use one of the following salutations:

- » Dear Sir or Madam

- » To whom it may concern

Closing Salutation
If you have addressed the recipient by name, your should conclude the letter with 'Yours sincerely', otherwise 'Yours faithfully' is appropriate.

Enclosures
As you will be enclosing your résumé or application form, you need to state their inclusion. You can either list all enclosed documents separately or just write 'Encl.' or 'Enclosures' below the signature line.

Attn

Sometimes the name of the addressee is preceded by attn (attention) or FAO (for the attention of), e.g. attn Ms Loren

Ms, Mrs or Miss

If you are writing to a woman and do not know if she uses Mrs or Miss, you can use Ms

Punctuation

In Britain, the salutation would be followed by either a comma, or no punctuation mark. In America, a colon is generally the accepted standard.

Proofread

As with any important document, absolutely no errors should be present. A typo, a poor printing job or a misspelling will create a poor impression.

Format

Cover letters should be written in standard business format and consist of a header, introduction, body and conclusion.

» Header
The header section consists of your return address, the date, recipients address and salutation.

» Introduction
The introduction explains your reason for contacting the company. If you are responding to an advertisement, refer to it and the source that published it.

» Body
The body briefly highlights what you have to offer and why you are suitable for the position. Don't let modesty prevent you from mentioning your strengths and don't simply repeat your résumé. Simply summarise the most relevant aspects that address the company's requirements directly..

You can also use the body of the letter to address gaps in your work history or other problems evident on your résumé. But do not draw attention to these unless you must, and never apologise. Always maintain a positive, confident tone.

» Conclusion
The conclusion sums up the letter and should be concise. Thank the reviewer, state your desire for an interview and indicate how you can be reached. If you intend to follow up with a phone call, state your intention to do so and then be sure you do it.

Going Digital

The fastest way to apply for employment is via email. However, with so much spam haunting our mailboxes it is also the fastest way to have your application trashed. To avoid being sent to the trash or spam box, stick to the simple guidelines that follow.

» Include an informative subject:
If you are responding to an advertisement, use the cited job title and job code. If you are making a speculative enquiry, put a few words stating your objective, for example: Jane Doe -- Résumé for beauty consultant position

» Send you résumé in the message body:
Paste a plain text version of your résumé right into the body of the message, immediately following your signature. This way, you avoid being automatically deleted by email systems that reject email attachments, and the recipient will have the benefit of seeing it as soon as he or she opens the message.

» Ensure proper email formatting
A hard return will sometimes produce two blank lines instead of
the one intended. Take the time to make sure your email looks
as good on all computers and in all email systems as it does on
your screen.

With regards to the content and layout, much of the conventional
cover letter guidelines apply, but with the obvious exceptions and
following alterations:

» Signature Block:
Much of the information that would be included in a header will
now become part of your signature. A signature is a block of text,
consisting of your name and contact details, which is appended
at the footer of your email message.

Signature blocks can be plain text or something fancier with
images and colours, however, a complex signature can become
illegible if the recipient has opted to receive email messages only
in plain text format.

Prepared Phrases

Introduction

» I would like to express my strong interest in the position of (position)
with (company)

» I am applying for the position of (position), which was advertised
(date) in (source)

» (Name) informed me of an opening for (position) that is available
at (company)

Body

» From my enclosed résumé, you will find that my experiences /
skills / ... align perfectly with the requirements you have outlined
for the position

» While my enclosed résumé provides a good overview of my
experiences / skills / ... I have also listed some specific skills that
meet your requirements for the position

» According to your advertisement, your position requires (skills).
These skills I have developed during ... (experience).

» I have more than ... years of ... experience.

» I am very competent in ...

Conclusion

- » I would welcome the opportunity to meet with you to discuss this position and my background in more detail

- » If you would like to schedule an interview, or otherwise discuss my interest in this position, you can reach me via my mobile on (telephone number) or via email (email address).

- » I will call you in a few days / next week / in early July / ... to discuss an interview.

- » I look forward to talking with you.

- » I look forward to hearing from you soon.

- » Thank you for your time and consideration.

- » Your consideration is greatly appreciated.

16 Any Road • Any Where
Any Town • AN8 9SE
United Kingdom
+44 (0)4587 875848 • Jane.Doe@Anymail.com

Attn: Ms Loren   25 February 2011
[Company]
23, Any Road
Any Where
Any Town
UNITED KINGDOM

Dear Ms Loren

I would like to express my strong interest in the position of [position] with [company], thus I have enclosed a copy of my résumé for your review and consideration.

As you will note, my enclosed résumé highlights my extensive eight years experience within the retail industry. Within which, I have built extensive customer relations, team working and supervisory experience, which have also greatly enhanced my communication and interpersonal skills.

With these skills and experiences combined with my passion for the industry, my motivation to succeed, strong attention to detail, and unparalleled work ethic, I am confident that I will make a positive contribution to the company and excel as a member of the [company] [position] team.

I would welcome the opportunity to meet with you to discuss this position and my background in more detail, and to explore the ways I could contribute to the ongoing success of your company.

If you would like to schedule an interview, or otherwise discuss my interest in this position, you can reach me on +44 (0) 4587 875 848 or via email Jane.Doe@Anymail.com

Thank you for your time and consideration. I look forward to hearing from you.

Yours sincerely,

Jane Doe
Encl

Figure 3. Cover Letter Sample

Subject: [Position] Opening - Reference: CC34873429

Dear Ms Loren

I would like to express my strong interest in the position of [position] with [company], thus I have attached a copy of my résumé for your review and consideration.

As you will note, my enclosed résumé highlights my extensive eight years experience within the retail industry. Within which, I have built extensive customer relations, team working and supervisory experience, which have also greatly enhanced my communication and interpersonal skills.

With these skills and experiences combined with my passion for the industry, my motivation to succeed, strong attention to detail, and unparalleled work ethic, I am confident that I will make a positive contribution to the company and excel as a member of the [company] [position] team.

I would welcome the opportunity to meet with you to discuss this position and my background in more detail, and to explore the ways I could contribute to the ongoing success of your company.

If you would like to schedule an interview, or otherwise discuss my interest in this position, you can reach me on +44 (0) 4587 875 848 or via email Jane.Doe@Anymail.com

Thank you for your time and consideration. I look forward to hearing from you.

Yours sincerely,
Jane Doe

Landline: +44 (0) 1577 385 927 | **Mobile:** +44 (0) 4587 875 848 | **Email:** Jane.Doe@Anymail.com
Address: 16 Any Road, Any Where , Any Town, AN8 9SE, UNITED KINGDOM

JANE DOE
16 Any Road • Any Where • Any Town • AN8 9SE • United Kingdom
+44 (0)4587 875848 • Jane.Doe@Anymail.com

OBJECTIVE
Seeking to pursue a [position] position with a company that rewards commitment and hard work, and offers opportunities to progress.

KEY SKILLS

Communication Skills:
Exhibits exceptional written and verbal communication skills, and is adept at communicating effectively with people at all levels, and in a manner appropriate to the audience.

Interpersonal Ability:
Unsurpassed interpersonal skills with a proven ability to quickly develop and maintain relationships with customers and colleagues.
...

Figure 4. E-Cover Letter Sample

Journal Notes

Create a Compelling CV/Résumé

CV vs Résumé

The main difference between a résumé and CV (Curriculum Vitae) is in the length. A CV is much more comprehensive than a résumé, which is generally brief.

A curriculum vitae is more commonly used In Europe, Asia, Africa and the Middle East.

Note:

For the sake of consistency, I will refer to this document as a résumé from this point forward

First and foremost, a résumé is used to enable employers to screen out unsuitable candidates. If successful through this initial screening stage, it will then be used to formulate suitable questions for the interview.

Because the recruiters will have no information about you beyond this document, it will be a major influence in the nature and direction of the interview. This allows an element of predictability and makes it a very powerful document indeed.

With such a valuable tool at your disposal, it is important that it represents the best you have to offer. If your résumé is strong, it will focus the recruiter's questioning on information that presents your image strongly. The following guidelines will help you achieve this.

Appearance

To retain consistency, you should continue the theme used for your cover letter (See page 59). When viewed as an entire package, it will create a very professional and consistent image. The exceptions are:

» Colour
Use colour sparingly. Black text, with a consistent injection of colour for the headings will make your resume more pleasing to the human eye, but photocopying may be problematic.

» Length
For this type of position, one or two pages is ideal. However, don't be constrained by this advice if doing so will mean that you have to squeeze your data in and use a tiny 8 point font, If you do find your résumé going beyond this quota, be sure that it isn't being filled with unnecessary, unfocused or excessive detail.

» Verso Printing
Double sided prints are harder to photocopy and risk show through. Stick to single sided prints for a cleaner look.

» Staples
Never staple your sheets together. Staples are inconvenient for the employer if they need to photocopy or scan your résumé, plus the reviewer may want to view the pages side by side. A traditional paper clip is acceptable.

» Identification
Be sure all of the pages include your name and page numbers so they can be easily reconnected should they become separated.

OCR Technology

To facilitate more efficient processing of résumés, some larger companies use a computerised tracking system. This system uses OCR (Optical Character Recognition) technology whereby incoming résumés are scanned as a graphic image, converted back into text, read and added to the database.

With this in mind, it is important to write and format your résumé in such a way that it can be successfully processed by these sophisticated systems. In this instance, the following guidelines apply:

Formatting
Simple formatting will yield the best results. So, avoid unnecessary and unreliable formatting such as italics, shading, and fancy fonts and stick to a simple one column, table less design using a standard typeface such as Georgia, Arial or Verdana.

Keywords
The system scans your résumé for keywords that indicate your skills, qualifications and experience. Following the scan, a score will be awarded based on the number of 'hits'. From this score, the system will either generate a letter of invitation, or a letter of rejection.

To ensure a high score, and an invitation letter, it is essential that you learn and inject as many keywords as possible throughout your résumé. The following highlighted keywords are the most widely scanned for:

» Good **communication** and **interpersonal** skills

» A **confident** and **friendly** personality

» Extensive **customer** service experience

» **Confidence** in dealing with a range of **people**

» The ability to work effectively in a **team**

» **Numeracy** skills for handling transactions

» Ability to handle **difficult customers** firmly and politely

» Ability to stay **calm**, **composed** and **focused** under **pressure**

» The ability to be **tactful** and **diplomatic**, but also **assertive** when necessary

Action Verbs

Action verbs express action. They are positive, powerful and directive, and should be used abundantly throughout your résumé.

Here are just a few examples:

» Communicated
» Conveyed
» Directed
» Explained
» Expressed
» Incorporated
» Interacted
» Listened
» Participated
» Persuaded
» Resolved
» Suggested
» Arranged
» Assisted
» Guided
» Provided
» Handled
» Generated
» Improved
» Trained

Consider the following sentence:
"As a hairdresser I had to carry out consultations with clients, which involved providing advice"

Now notice how using direct action verbs makes the sentence much more powerful:
"As a hairdresser, I consulted with clients and provided advice"

A full list of action verbs can be found on page 87

Format

There are three basic résumé formats:

» Chronological:
The chronological résumé highlights the dates, places of employment and job titles, and is most effective for candidates who have a strong, solid work history. It is less effective for those who want to disguise gaps in employment or frequent job changes.

» Functional:
A functional résumé focuses on skills and experience rather than work history. Its ability to accentuate your transferable skills and detract attention from your career history makes it better suited to those who want to downplay an extreme career change or a chequered employment history. This style is less useful if you have limited work experience as there will be little to highlight.

» Combination:
The combination résumé, as the name implies, is a combination of the chronological and functional formats. It highlights both your work history and your transferable skills, and is most effective when you have a great deal of transferable skills and a solid work history.

The chronological format is most preferred by employers, followed closely by the combination format. The functional format is the least effective.

Outline

For the purpose of a customer service position, I have listed possible résumé sections below, in suggested order:

Applicant Information
At the beginning of the résumé, include your name, your home mailing address, your telephone number(s), and your e-mail address. If you have both temporary and permanent addresses, include them both.

Objective Statement (Optional)
An objective is a short statement which defines your career goals. It gives your résumé focus and shows that you have given consideration to your career direction.

Examples: Seeking to utilise extensive customer service experience and exceptional communicative ability within a support manager role.

Seeking to pursue a receptionist position with a company that rewards commitment and hard work, and offers opportunities to progress.

Key Skills (Optional)
The key skills section provides a fantastic opportunity for you to quickly express your suitability for the role and show what transferable skills your will bring to the position. Additionally, it will bulk out your résumé with the keywords needed for OCR scanning technology (See page 68).

Key skills to consider are: Communication Skills
Interpersonal Ability
Customer Focus
Team Player
Problem Solver
Leadership

Employment History (Chronological & Combination Formats)
Your employment history should be displayed in reverse chronological order, that is starting with your most recent position and working backwards, and include: the name of the organisation, the position held, the period of employment, the duties performed and results achieved.

The period of employment should include both the start and end dates, and can consist of only the month and year.

Tip:

If you include an objective, focus your attention on what you can do for the employer, not what the employer can do for you.

Note:

While an objective is optional, it is important if you are changing fields, are a graduate or an entry-level job seeker, or have a diverse employment history.

Tip:

Don't limit your key skills to those gained through work experience. Consider skills you have gained from your hobbies, during studies, and voluntary placements.

Note:

Employment
Employment history is a broad term that can include relevant internships, summer or seasonal jobs, part time work, and voluntary placements. This is especially important if you have little paid experience.

When describing your duties use action phrases, rather than compete sentences or generic job descriptions, and list any accomplishments which back up any key skill statements that you have made. For example, if you have stated 'extensive leadership experience' you can use a short action statement such as: "Supervised and trained a team of four junior-level stylists". Three to five of these statements are ideal.

If some entries are more relevant to the position, emphasise these and provide only summaries for those of less significance.

Education Summary
Starting with the most recent and working backwards, include the schools/colleges/universities you have attended. Within each entry, include the year of completion ("In progress" or "expected" are acceptable, if necessary) and award(s) you achieved.

Certifications (Optional)
If you have attended any formal certification courses, e.g., First aid, life saving, then list the details here noting the institution name, date and certification awarded.

Activities and Interests (Optional)
Recreational interests reveal a great deal about your personality and create depth to your character. They also serve as excellent sources of additional skills and experiences, which can be advantageous if you lack certain skills and/or experience.

Generalised list statements such as: 'reading, watching television, sport and socialising' are not only bland, they are also too common. Additionally, a statement such as: 'I enjoy spending time with my mates, hitting the town and going out on the razz" lacks variety, doesn't highlight any key skills, and sounds very unprofessional.

Instead, use something such as: 'I have been a keen footballer for as long as I can remember and am an active member of Anytown women's football club where I have been captain of the team for 3 years. I have an active interest in nature, and regularly get involved with and manage conservation assignments. To relax, I attend yoga and meditation classes, which help to keep me focused and relieve stress.'

This statement gives an immediate impression of someone who is balanced and committed. Their interests highlight several admirable qualities such as team spirit and leadership, and it also details their methods of stress management. A recruitment officer would form a positive impression of the candidate based on a statement such as this.

Jane Doe

Seeking to pursue
a consultant
position
with a company
that rewards
commitment and
hard work, and
offers opportunities
to progress.

Key Skills

Communication Skills
Exhibits exceptional written and verbal communication skills, and is adept at communicating effectively with people at all levels, and in a manner appropriate to the audience.

Interpersonal Ability
Unsurpassed interpersonal skills with a proven ability to quickly develop and maintain relationships with customers and colleagues.

Customer Focus
Experienced at providing a high quality service to customers at all levels, and skilled at effectively dealing with and resolving complaints.

Team Spirited
Skilled team player who adapts quickly to different team dynamics and excels at building trusting relationships with colleagues at all levels.

Problem Solver
Creative thinker who applies logic and initiative to difficult situations.

Employment History

Freelance Hairdresser   Feb '03 - Present
» Manage and maintain a customer base of over 100 clients
» Consult and advise customers
» Ensure customer satisfaction
» Provide a friendly and professional service
» Maintain up to date records and accounts

Trina's Hair Salon | Senior Stylist   Aug '00 – Feb '03
» Supervised and trained a team of four junior-level stylists
» Hired work experience students
» Consulted and advised customers
» Ensured customer comfort and satisfaction
» Provided a friendly and professional service

16 Any Road • Any Where
Any Town • AN8 9SE
United Kingdom

+44 (0)4587 875848
Jane.Doe@Anymail.com

Figure 5. Sample Combination Résumé Page 1

Jane Doe

Continued from page 1...

My confident and
friendly nature
will enable me to
fit in and
complement
your existing team

Employment History

Trina's Hair Salon - Junior Stylist   April '98 – Aug '00
» Consulted and advised customers
» Ensured customer comfort and satisfaction
» Provided a friendly and professional service

Macey's Hair Salon - Receptionist   July '96 – April '98
» Delivered the highest level of customer service
» Ensured customer comfort
» Provided a friendly and professional service
» Assisted with enquiries and resolved complaints

Education Summary

Any College (2001)   NVQ 3 - Hairdressing
Any College (1999)   NVQ 2 - Hairdressing
Any College (1998)   NVQ 1 – Hairdressing
Any High School (1996)   11 GCSE's (grade A–D)

Certifications

British Red Cross   Basic First Aid – Sept '06

Languages

Fluent in spoken and written Spanish
Basic conversational ability in French

Activities & Interests

I have been a keen footballer for as long as I can remember and
am an active member of Any Town women's football club where I
have been captain of the team for 3 years. I have an active interest
in nature and regularly get involved with and manage conservation
assignments. To relax, I attend yoga and meditation classes that help
to keep me focused and relieve stress.

16 Any Road • Any Where
Any Town • AN8 9SE
United Kingdom

+44 (0)4587 875848
Jane.Doe@Anymail.com

References

Written references are available on request

Figure 6. Sample Combination Résumé Page 2

Going Digital

Résumés can be formatted for digital distribution by using a universally friendly format such as:

Plain Text Format (.txt)
Plain text format is the simplest of the three formats. As the name suggests, it is stripped of virtually all of its formatting and, as a result, is not particularly visually appealing. Functionality wise it is without limitations as it is completely cross compatible and virus free. You can attach it to an email, embed it within the body of an email message, or use it to cut and paste into online forms.

To create a .txt file, simply open your résumé in a word processing program . Save the file using 'Save as' and select file type: Text only (*.txt).

Rich Text Format (.rtf)
Rich text résumés can be created using word processing software, such as Microsoft Word, and saved as .rtf format. The formatting within this style is much more visually pleasing than the plain text format, however, complex formatting may look strange when opened in different software on different computers. The solution is to keep it simple by avoiding unusual fonts and excessive formatting.

This format works well as an attachment when accompanied by a text version that is pasted within the e-cover letter.

Portable Document Format (.pdf)
The PDF format is probably the most versatile format of the three as it is completely cross compatible, virus free, and retains all its original formatting regardless of the computer it is viewed on. As such, it has a clean and professional appearance.

You can convert your word processed résumé into a PDF document by using the following software:

» OpenOffice Writer

» Microsoft Office Word

» Cute PDF Writer

» PDF Creator

Note:

Before proceeding with any one format, you should note that some email systems will automatically reject e-mails that contain attachments. So, proceed with caution.

Sending your résumé via email

You can send your résumé by embedding it within the text of the email or attaching it as an external attachment.

To embed your résumé within the email message, simply copy and paste it into the body of the message.

If, however, you intend to send your résumé as an email attachment the following guidelines should be followed:

» Use your name, or some variation, as the filename. For instance: "janedoe-resume.pdf" or "j.doe.pdf"

» Avoid password protection

» Test, test and test again. Send it to a friend or two first to make sure it works as it should

JANE DOE

16 Any Road • Any Where • Any Town • AN8 9SE • United Kingdom
+44 (0)4587 875848 • Jane.Doe@Anymail.com

OBJECTIVE

Seeking to pursue a customer relations position with a company that rewards commitment and hard work, and offers opportunities to progress.

KEY SKILLS

Communication Skills:
Exhibits exceptional written and verbal communication skills, and is adept at communicating effectively with people at all levels, and in a manner appropriate to the audience.

Interpersonal Ability:
Unsurpassed interpersonal skills with a proven ability to quickly develop and maintain relationships with customers and colleagues.

Customer Focus:
Experienced at providing a high quality service to customers at all levels, and skilled at effectively dealing with and resolving complaints.

Team Player:
Skilled team player who adapts quickly to different team dynamics and excels at building trusting relationships with colleagues at all levels.

Problem Solver:
Creative thinker who applies logic and initiative to difficult situations.

...

Figure 7. Plain Text Résumé Sample

Journal Notes

Prepare a Powerful Application

Job applications are primarily used to collect data from potential applicants for the purpose of evaluating their skills, qualifications, employment history and motives. Unlike résumés, which are unique to each individual, its standardised format allows selectors to quickly peruse each form and screen out any unsuitable candidates.

From the company's perspective, the form also serves a number of other purposes. Namely: To evaluate the applicant's literacy, ability to follow instructions, penmanship and communication skills. A careless applicant, or one who doesn't follow instructions, will quickly disqualify themselves.

Quick Tips

Before you Begin

» Photocopy the blank form

» Read through the form to familiarise yourself with the questions and any specific instructions

» Gather materials: Black pens, a pencil and eraser

» Gather the necessary information:
  Personal details: Passport, contact information, vital statistics
  Education and training information: Qualifications, dates, results
  Employment History: Names, addresses, key dates

» Plan what you want to write in each section, taking note of the space available

» Practice on the photocopied forms, or use blank sheets of paper

» Walk away for a few hours and return with a fresh pair of eyes

» Proofread and make any necessary adjustments: Be mindful of typos, grammatical errors and inaccuracies

Completing the Form

» Set aside sufficient time and minimise distractions

» Follow instructions

» Use black ink

» Write clearly and neatly: Block capitals are tidy and easy to read

» Keep your text within the space provided

» Answer every question and use 'Not Applicable' or 'N/A' where questions are not relevant to you

» Keep the tone positive and don't volunteer negative information

» Be concise

» Avoid continuations on separate sheets of paper if you can. If unavoidable, remember to clearly state your name and detail which part of the application form it is linked to

Finishing Off

» Complete a final proofread

» Make a copy of the final form for future reference

» Select an envelope that is large enough not to require any folding of the form

» Address the envelope correctly and apply the correct postage

» Send it off before the closing date

Guidance Notes

Employment History

Unless requested otherwise, your employment history should be displayed in reverse chronological order, that is starting with your most recent position and working backwards,

When describing your duties (as noted on page 70) three to five action phrases have a better impact than complete sentences or generic job descriptions. Consider the following examples:

» 'As a call centre officer, I answer customer queries and complaints over the telephone'

» 'Address customer queries and resolve complaints'

The former example has a passive tone and is unnecessarily wordy. The latter example, on the other hand, still uses the important key words, but uses an active and punchy tone.

Faux Pas Alert

Consider the following examples.

> I currently work as a freelance hairdresser and have worked in client facing roles for more than 8 years. I am looking for a change in my life direction and feel that a career as BEAUTY CONSULTANT will give me this.

> I curently work as freelance hairdresser & have worked in client facing roles fore more than 8 years. I am looking for a change in my life direction and feel that that a career as beauty consutant will give me th

The first example is tidy and creates an positive impression of the candidate. Meanwhile, the second example is messy, full of typos and barely legible. It is clear that the candidate jumped straight in without planning. Hardly a positive first impression.

Note:

Due to the self explanatory nature of the majority of questions, only those that require additional guidance will be elaborated on further.

Past or Present Tense?

If it was a previous job, then use the past tense (initiated, facilitated, answered). If it is a current position, then use the present tense (assist, identify, create).

Most importantly, you must communicate your suitability for the position clearly by highlighting the skills and experience that are relevant and transferable. For example, a salon receptionist may include the following:

» Delivered the highest level of customer service

» Ensured customer comfort

» Provided a friendly and professional service

» Assisted with enquiries and resolved complaints

This active statement identifies customer contact experience, as well as other specific responsibilities and attributes that are required for customer service roles. It would be clear to any company that this candidate has the necessary experience and is clearly suited for the position.

» Irrelevant positions
Where a position holds little or no relevance, short summaries are acceptable. If those positions were very brief, dated, or only part time, you may be able to safely exclude their inclusion altogether. You should only do so, however, if doing so will not create damaging gaps.

» Lack of relative experience
If you lack experience, you should certainly get some. Whether you take on a short term voluntary post at a local charity shop or some weekend bar work, you will surely strengthen your application.

» Fragmented work history
A fragmented job history, one that is made up of lots of short-term jobs, will not present a favourable impression to a potential employer. Fortunately, there are several options you can consider which will minimise its impact:

A process of elimination
If eliminating brief, dated, irrelevant, or part time jobs will not create damaging gaps, you should consider doing so

Spring into summer
Instead of listing specific dates for summer jobs, you can simply state Summer 20xx to Spring 20xx.

Consecutive combining
Where several similar consecutive jobs appear, you can combine them into one chunk, for example:

2004–2006	Receptionist Aztec Hotel & Spa, Bloomfields Leisure, Trina's Hair & Beauty Salon

» Gaps in employment
If you have gaps in your employment history, you may be asked to elaborate on these. Whatever your reasons: maternity leave, study or travel break, be honest and positive, and be prepared to discuss the details openly.

If you were doing anything during the gaps, paid or unpaid, it would be ideal to insert them into your work history to fill the gaps.

For example:

2005–2009	Full Time Parent
Summer 2004–Spring 2005	Travelled around Europe

» Career progression
If you have remained with an employer for several years but have progressed through the ranks, you can make your progression more obvious by listing each position as you would a new job.

» Reasons for leaving
While your reason for leaving your current employment is probably for career advancement, you should consider expanding on this, if space permits, to make it more memorable. For example:

"To advance my career as a cruise attendant with a company that I admire"

Your reasons for leaving your previous employment may be for any reason: career advancement, not enough hours, wider responsibilities, temporary contract, redundancy, maternity leave, study break, travel break, or company relocation. Whatever your reason, remain positive and avoid phrases such as fired, terminated, quit, illness and personal reasons,

If you were fired or quit under less than favourable conditions, avoid drawing attention to the fact by using neutral phrases such as 'job ended'. Alternatively, you can simply state 'Will explain at the interview'. Both of these will provide you with the opportunity to discuss the details openly at interview where you can create a more favourable and detailed response.

Remember, you should not lie about your reasons for leaving previous employment posts as they are grounds for dismissal in the future.

Awards

Outstanding excellence will show commitment and talent, so if you have achieved any awards through your activities, be sure to list them. Make sure the achievements are recent, though, as outdated awards may give the impression that you haven't achieved anything since.

Stretching the Truth

Don't be tempted to just tell them what you think they want to hear. Exaggerations or untruths can come back to haunt you if you're are quizzed about them at the interview, or even later in employment. Be equally mindful about over indulging as the recruiter may get the impression that your hobbies will take priority over your work.

Balancing Act

To achieve balance, list a mix of individual pursuits and group activities.

Leisure Interests

As noted on page 71, recreational interests create depth and humanises your character. A targeted list, which focuses on relevant skills, will form an immediate and positive impression. They also serve as excellent sources of additional skills and experiences, which can be advantageous if you lack employment experience.

Generalised list statements such as: 'reading, watching television, sport and socialising' should be avoided, as should unprofessional statements such as: 'I enjoy spending time with my mates, hitting the town and going out on the razz".

To enhance your application form positively, focus and expand on those interests that have some relevance to the position. For instance, being captain of a football team demonstrates leadership qualities, while volunteering at a local charity indicates good people skills.

Here is an example: 'I have been a keen footballer for as long as I can remember and am an active member of Any Town women's football club where I have been captain of the team for 3 years. I have an active interest in nature, and regularly get involved with and manage conservation assignments. To relax, I attend yoga and meditation classes, which help to keep me focused and relieve stress.'

This statement gives an immediate impression of someone who is balanced and committed. Their interests highlight several admirable qualities such as team spirit and leadership, and it also details their methods of stress management. A recruitment office would form a positive impression of the candidate based on a statement such as this.

References

Always get permission from the person(s) you state as your referee(s) and give them a copy of your application form or résumé to help them write a relevant reference that highlights your most important points.

If you don't have any work references that you can use, you should provide a character reference instead. This can be a school teacher, university lecturer or a friend in an authoritative position such as a police officer or doctor.

If you have been fired, or you resigned under less than favourable circumstances, you may want to call the employer to find out what they would say in response to reference checks. Usually, past employers will agree to use the term 'resigned' if you explain that your termination is hurting your chances of finding employment.

Additional Information / Personal Statement

At the end of most application forms, you will be presented with some form of additional information box. This box may simply state 'Additional Information', or it could be more specific, such as:

» Please state your reason for applying and why you feel you are suited to the position

» Please provide further information which you feel will benefit your application

Essentially, this is an opportunity to sell yourself and you should use it to provide a power statement which summarises your experience, highlights your key skills, and shares your motives all within a few short paragraphs.

Consider the following example:

'As you will note, I have eight years experience within the retail industry. Within which, I have built extensive customer relations, team working and supervisory experience, which has also greatly enhanced my communication and interpersonal skills.

With these skills and experiences, combined with my passion for the industry, my motivation to succeed, strong attention to detail, and unparalleled work ethic, I am confident that I will make a positive contribution to the company and excel as a member of the [company] [position] team.

I would welcome the opportunity to meet with you to discuss this position and my background in more detail, and to explore the ways I could contribute to the ongoing success of your company.'

The above example is concise. It focuses on what the candidate can offer the company, rather than what the company can offer the candidate, and it showcases skills and experiences that are an asset for the applied position.

Zika Hair & Beauty

Application for Employment

All information supplied will be treated as confidential.
Subject to meeting the eligibility criteria, you will be invited to attend our next selection day.
Correct information will be a condition of employment.

Full Name (Mr / Mrs / (Ms))   JANE DOE   Date Available   29/01/11

Present Address	Permanent Address (If different)
22 Any Street Any TowN ANY WHERE	N/A

Post Code	AN2 6DG	Country	U.K	Post Code	N/A	Country	N/A

Please give telephone numbers in the format: Country Code + City/Mobile Code + Phone Number

Telephone (Residence)	44 1179 637264	Telephone (Residence)	N/A
Telephone (Mobile)	44 798 837472	Telephone (Mobile)	N/A
Email	Jane.doe@anymail.com		

Education   Please continue on a separate sheet if necessary

From	To	Name & Address of School/College	Subject(s)	Results
09/99	07/01	Any college - any where - an8 7kd	hairdressing	nvq 3 - distinction
09/98	07/99	Any college - any where - an8 7kd	hairdressing	nvq 2 - merit
09/97	07/98	Any college - any where - an8 7kd	hairdressing	nvq 1 - distinction
09/91	07/96	any school - any where - an8 375	english / geography french / art / cdt maths / science / maths	8 gcse's grade a-c

Figure 8. Sample Application Form - Page 1

Present/Last Employer

Employer:	Self employed	From: 01/02/03	To: Present
Position:	Hairdresser	Salary:	15,000 pa
Address:	n/a	Notice Required:	None
		Reason for Leaving:	To pursue a career as MAKEUP ARTIST

Responsibilities:
Manage and maintain a customer base of over 100 clients
Consult and advise customers
Ensure customer satisfaction
Provide a friendly and professional service
Maintain up to date records and accounts

Previous Employment   Please continue on a separate sheet if necessary

Employer:	Trina's hair salon	From: 16/02/00	To: 01/02/03
Address:	159 Any city centre any town - an9 6dj	Responsibilities:	Supervised and trained a team of four junior-level stylists - Hired work experience students - Consulted and advised customers - Ensured customer comfort and satisfaction - Provided a friendly and professional service
Position	senior hair stylist		
Reason for Leaving:	to pursue freelance opportunity		

Employer:	Trina's hair salon	From: 05/04/98	To: 16/08/00
Address:	159 Any city centre any town - an9 6dj	Responsibilities:	Consulted and advised customers - Ensured customer comfort and satisfaction - Provided a friendly and professional service
Position	junior hair stylist		
Reason for Leaving:	to pursue promotion opportunity		

Employer:	MACEY's hair salon	From: 24/07/97	To: 05/04/98
Address:	378 Any city centre any town - an5 6sj	Responsibilities:	Delivered the highest level of customer service - Ensured customer comfort - Provided a friendly and professional service - Assisted with enquiries and resolved complaints
Position	receptionist		
Reason for Leaving:	to pursue promotion opportunity		

Please explain any gaps in unemployment
upon leaving school in 1996, i spent a year travelling before moving into employment

Please list any voluntary work
For the last three years, i have volunteered at the samaritans homeless shelter during the christmas period, where i help cook and serve beverages

Figure 9. Sample Application Form - Page 2

Additional Training
Give details of any first aid and/or nursing qualifications

british red cross - basic first aid training - 09/2006

Give details of languages spoken and abilities

English - native language
french - read, write and speak fluently
spanish - basic conversational ability

Give details of any other training

i have attended, and passed, short courses in leadership and communication

---

Hobbies/Outside Interests

I have been a keen footballer for as long as I can remember and am an active member of Any Town women's football club where I have been captain of the team for 3 years. I have an active interest in nature and regularly get involved with and manage conservation assignments. To relax, I attend yoga and meditation classes that help to keep me focused and relieve stress.

Use the following space to provide any further information that you feel will benefit your application

As you will note, I have an extensive eight years experience within the retail industry. Within these roles, I have built extensive customer relations, team working and supervisory experience, and greatly enhanced my communication and interpersonal skills.

With these skills and experiences, combined with my passion for the industry, my motivation to succeed, strong attention to detail, and unparalleled work ethic, I am confident that I will make a positive contribution to the company and excel as a member of the team.

Declaration
Have you ever been convicted of a criminal offence which, at the date of application, is not a spent conviction as defined in the Rehabilitation of Offenders Act 1974?   Yes/No
If yes, then such convictions must be disclosed below.

n/a

The details provided on this application are correct to my knowledge and belief. I understand that my application may be rejected or that I may be dismissed for withholding relevant information or giving false information. I am aware that my employment with ABC Company will be subject to satisfactory references.

Signature   Date   05/01/2011

Figure 10.   Sample Application Form - Page 3

Going Digital

The only significant difference between a digital application form and its paper counterpart is how they are completed. The questions will be similar and both require the same effort. Before you proceed, here are some useful pointers for you to follow:

» Be prepared
Before you proceed with the online form, have an up to date résumé to hand so that you have relevant details in front of you for reference.

» Offline drafting
The benefit of using a word processing package to draft and save you answers is threefold. Firstly, you will have a back up if any problems occur with the online form. Secondly, you will be able to run a spell check before you copy the information into the online system. Thirdly, your information will not be lost if your session times out (See the note below).

» Follow the instructions
The online system should guide you through the process, so follow any instructions carefully. In most cases there will be a help button if you get really stuck.

» Keep a record
Most online forms offer the option of storing your application for later completion or revision. If you choose to do this, be sure to keep a record of any user names and passwords so that you can sign back in.

» Time out
Some online application forms have a time out facility, whereby the session will close after a period of inactivity. If a system such as this is in place, there will usually be a timer displayed. However, this may not always be the case so you should always save your progress.

» Submission
Don't press the submit button until you have backed up your answers, proofread the application form and are 100% happy with your entries. Once it has been submitted, you can't reverse the submission.

Preparation Essentials

Personal Information
» Contact information (telephone number, email, fax)

Education and Training Details
» Names and addresses of institutions
» Qualifications and results
» Dates

Career History
» Names of employers
» Dates
» Reference details

Action Verbs

Achieved	Enlisted	Organised
Addressed	Established	Originated
Advocated	Evaluated	Overhauled
Allocated	Examined	Oversaw
Analysed	Executed	Performed
Anticipated	Expedited	Persuaded
Appraised	Fabricated	Pioneered
Approved	Facilitated	Planned
Arbitrated	Forecasted	Presented
Arranged	Formulated	Produced
Assembled	Founded	Projected
Assessed	Generated	Promoted
Attained	Guided	Publicised
Authored	Handled	Recommended
Balanced	Identified	Recruited
Budgeted	Illustrated	Reduced
Built	Implemented	Referred
Calculated	Improved	Repaired
Catalogued	Increased	Reported
Clarified	Influenced	Represented
Classified	Informed	Researched
Coached	Initiated	Resolved
Collaborated	Inspected	Review
Collected	Instituted	Reviewed
Compiled	Integrated	Revitalised
Conceptualized	Interpreted	Scheduled
Consolidated	Interviewed	Shaped
Consulted	Introduced	Solved
Contracted	Invented	Spearheaded
Convinced	Investigated	Spoke
Coordinated	Lectured	Strengthened
Corresponded	Led	Summarised
Counselled	Listened	Supervised
Created	Litigated	Systematised
Critiqued	Maintained	Taught
Customised	Marketed	Trained
Delegated	Mediated	Translated
Demonstrated	Moderated	Upgrades
Designed	Motivated	Wrote
Developed	Negotiated	
Directed	Operated	

Journal Notes

Surpass the Telephone Screening

In a quest to save time and money, some companies are now adopting telephone screening techniques. The telephone screening allows selectors to determine a candidate's eligibility, and then eliminate unsuitable candidates without going to the expense of inviting them to attend an interview.

The information you supply at this stage is vital to your continuation in the process so you need to be prepared. Thus, I have devised the following guidelines to give you the best chance of success.

Format

Telephone screenings vary between company's and, generally, come in two formats:

» Quick and general
  This style of screening is usually straightforward and consists of a series of simple questions which seek to identify eligibility. For example: Do you have customer service experience? Are you qualified?

» Deep and detailed
  This format is more comparable to a formal interview and you can expect tougher elimination questions. For example: Why do you want to work for us? Why do you want the job? Tell me about your weaknesses?

Be Prepared

As soon as you submit a résumé or application form, you should be prepared to receive a call from a recruiter, at any time. Although you cannot control the timing of these calls, there are some precautions you can take to ensure that you are not caught completely off guard.

Outgoing voice mail
For times when you are unable to take a call, a professional outgoing voice mail message will provide the best impression. For example:

"Hello. You have reached Jane Doe's voice mail. I'm sorry I am unable to take your call at present, but please leave your name, telephone number and a short message, and I'll be sure to return your call as soon as possible".

Mobile telephone usage

Where possible, your first choice of contact should be via a land-line telephone. If a mobile phone is unavoidable, however, make sure it has a clear sound and you maintain a full battery.

Prepare for potential questions

To ensure that you can provide precise answers to the recruiter's questions, you should have your résumé in front of you.

Some questions you might expect in a telephone screening are:

» Can you tell me about yourself and your work history?

» Why are you leaving your present job?

» Why do you want to work for us?

» What interests you about this job?

» What skills can you bring to the position?

You should also be ready to provide some specific examples of accomplishments and experiences which showcase your customer service and teamwork skills.

Take notes

Keep a pen and paper on hand so that you can write down brief notes about the call, including the callers name and phone number.

If you are offered to attend a formal interview, make a note of the date and time, the location and phone number, and directions to the venue (if offered).

Keep hydrated

Depending on the length of the conversation, and how nervous you become, a dry mouth and throat can become a hazard. For this reason, I would suggest sipping on a glass of water throughout the telephone call.

Make a Positive Impression

Returning missed calls

Return missed calls promptly and be prepared to interview immediately.

If you reach the recruiter's voice mail, you should leave a message using the following guidelines:

» Speak slowly and clearly
It goes without saying that the recipient should hear and understand every word.

Speak Clearly

Make a conscious effort to slow the pace of your speech and enunciate clearly. Speaking too fast, too close to the mouthpiece or mumbling will make you harder to understand.

Use Silence

It is easy to talk too much when you are nervous. A moment of silence, while it might seem awkward to you, lets the recruiter know that you are done.

Read more about communication on page 48

» Avoid filler words
Filler words, such as ums and ahs, sound unprofessional. Avoid their use by preparing your message in advance.

» Introduce yourself
Begin the message by introducing yourself and identifying for who the message is for. Example: "Hello. This is a message from Jane Doe for Carrie Loren"

» Leave a short summary message
A short summary detailing your reason for calling is sufficient, such as: "I received your message regarding the [position] selection interview and would be eager to discuss the position with you further"

» Close the message
End the call by stating your availability and telephone number(s). For instance: "You can reach me on 01137 483 948 Monday to Friday between 9 and 5, or on my mobile 07897 786 897 from 5 onwards. I look forward to speaking with you shortly".

Use the recruiter's name
To establish rapport, write down the recruiter's name and use it throughout the conversation.

Dress the part
If you are initiating the call, or if you know to expect one, you should make an effort to dress appropriately. This doesn't necessarily mean full business attire, but it does mean something that will make you feel relaxed, yet alert and businesslike. Slacks or a bathrobe will hardly make you feel professional, and it certainly won't put you in the correct frame of mind for a formal telephone conversation.

Keep an upright posture
To give your voice more energy and projection power, try maintaining a good upright posture.

Pay attention to your tone
Your voice plays a key role in sending the correct messages. If your tone sounds bored and distracted, it won't matter how enthusiastically you phrase your answers because your tone will be the message that sticks with the recruiter. The key is to match the sound of your voice to the words you are using.

To check the level of enthusiasm in your voice, you can practice with a tape recorder.

Ask for clarification

If you are unsure or feel you have misunderstood a question, it is better to request the recruiter to repeat, rephrase or summarise the question than to answer the question incorrectly.

Rather than jump straight in with your question, though, you should consider using a polite introductory phrase, such as:

» I beg your pardon, but I don't quite follow/understand. I wonder if you could rephrase that in a different way?

» Do you think you could repeat the part about ... once again please?

» Pardon me. Would you mind repeating that?

» Sorry, but I'm not sure I'm following you.

» Let's see if I understand/understood you correctly ...

» Do you/Does this mean that...

» Would it be correct to say that...

» So in other words...

Faux Pas Alerts

Leading or controlling

Don't try to lead or control the conversation, this is the recruitment officer's Job. You can, however, ask questions of your own when opportunities arise.

Distractions & Interruptions

Minimise potential distractions by taking the call in a quiet room. If you are caught at an inopportune time, politely ask the caller to hold for a brief moment while you move to a quiet location. You could say "Could you give me a moment to go to a room where we won't be interrupted?"

Alternatively, if the timing is really bad, you can respectfully request an alternative date and time by saying "I do apologise, but is there a time I can reach you later? I'm very interested in the position and want to give you my undivided attention, but I'm afraid that now isn't the best time."

Interrupting the recruiter

Unless absolutely necessary, you should never interrupt the recruiter while they are speaking. Write down any questions or comments you have for later.

Verbal Cues

Although you should never interrupt the recruiter, you shouldn't listen in total silence either. Instead, use verbal feedback cues to indicate that you are listening and that you understand. This will encourage the recruiter to continue.

Some verbal feedback signals include:

» "uh huh"
» "I see."
» "Yes"
» "Ok"
» "I understand"
» "That's interesting"
» "Sure"
» "Right"
» "Of course"

Smile

A smile will add warmth to your voice and make it sound friendly, inviting and enthusiastic. To give yourself a boost, there are several things you can do:

» Keep a humorous, inspirational or special picture nearby
» Keep a mirror in front of you as a reminder to smile
» Think about someone you care about
» Have a funny joke pinned up
» Have some happy music playing in the background (make sure it is appropriate music though and not too loud)

Negativity

There is no room for negativity when it comes to interviews of any kind. Be especially careful when discussing other jobs, company's, people, previous employers and your current job.

Puff Puff, Slurp Slurp

Any sounds you make close to the receiver will be amplified at the other end so avoid smoking, eating and drinking close to the mouthpiece.

Umm, Anyways

Anyways, you know how when you are, like, really nervous, and you ,ummm, find it hard to verbalise and stuff and you say silly things that, kind of, make you sound, like, kind of, unprofessional and maybe, like, inarticulate?

The useless and annoying verbal mannerisms used in the above example "you know," "like," "in other words," "kind of," "ummm," and "anyways." should be avoided at all costs. Besides making you sound unprofessional, they also detract attention from your message.

Unprepared or unnecessary questions

To stand out as an informed and competent applicant, your questions should reflect that you have researched the company and the position. Asking questions that have already been addressed within the company's literature will make you appear unprepared and incompetent.

Likewise, asking questions that are based on money and benefits will make you appear selfishly motivated and give a negative impression about your motives for the position and/or the company.

Making a Successful Close

As the recruitment officer begins to conclude the interview thank him or her for their time and, if they haven't suggested an in person interview, enquire about the next steps and tell them that you are available for a face-to-face interview.

For example: "I've really enjoyed talking to you and am very interested in the position. What are the next steps in the hiring process? Should I expect to hear from you soon?"

Journal Notes

Concluding Notes

Proofreading Checklist

When proofreading your work, be mindful of:

» Spellings and typos
» Grammar and punctuation
» Factuality
» Sentence structure
» Logic
» Consistency of word usage

Proofread, Proofread, Proofread

The importance of proofreading your documents cannot be emphasised enough. Mistakes in grammar, punctuation and spelling reflect badly on your effort and may be the excuse a selector needs when trying to 'thin the pack'.

With so much importance resting on the final presentation, I have devised a list of guidelines to assist you in proofreading your work:

» Use a spell checker
The built in spell checker within most word processing programs can help you catch some basic errors such as, repeated words and reversed letters. Don't rely too heavily on these, however, as they are by no means perfect.

» Give it a rest
If time allows, set aside your work for at least a few hours. When you return, you will have fresh eyes and will be able to spot errors much more efficiently.

» Prepare
Proofreading requires concentration, patience, and time. Proofread at a time when you are most alert, not rushed and less likely to be distracted.

» Use a checklist
If there are words that you regularly misspell or misuse, make a note of these and cross reference them each time you proofread.

» Review a hard copy
Reviewing your work in an alternative format may reveal errors that you may have otherwise missed.

» Break it down
Rather than carrying out one large proofread, break the process down into smaller, specific proofreads. For instance, use the first pass for spelling, the second for punctuation, the third for grammar, and so on.

» Slowly does it
Proofread each paragraph one by one, sentence by sentence, word by word.

» Work backwards
Working backwards through the text is the best way to catch spelling errors as it focuses your mind on the individual words, rather than the context of a complete sentence.

» Use your ears
One of the best ways to edit and proofread your work is to read it out loud. Missing words, lack of clarity, or even phrasing that just doesn't sound quite right, can be picked up better when read aloud.

» Seek assistance
A new set of eyes will certainly spot some errors that you have overlooked, so invite a friend or relative to assist you in the process.

Journal Notes

Attend

Introduction

What to Expect

More and more companies are adopting group practical elements to their selection process. As such, there is no set formula as to how many or which combination of activities will be included during any interview.

There are three key segments that you may encounter, these are: Group activities, individual assessments and a formal interview.

» Group activities
   During a group interview, you may be asked to take part in several activities. These activities are designed to reveal your personality, competencies and potential for working within the position. There are likely to be a series of practical tasks, group discussions and role plays.

» Individual assessments
   Individual assessments may be paper based, such as personality questionnaires and general knowledge tests, or they may be practical, such as a self presentation.

» Formal interview
   A formal interview will typically take place before one recruitment officer, but may extend to two or more. In a panel scenario, it is common practice to have a primary examiner to ask questions and a secondary examiner to observe and take notes.

Attendance
The volume of attendees will depend on the company and the assessment procedure. Typically, assessment days will accommodate fewer than 30 candidates.

Venue
Invitation only assessments and final interviews are typically held at the company's own premises. Open days attract a larger attendance so will commonly be held within a hotel establishment.

Schedule
The assessment process varies considerably in length and structure depending on a number of factors. In some instances, they may span only a few short hours. In other cases, they may be split over a series of days. Your invitation letter or the company's website will provide further confirmation of the predicted schedule.

For reference, panel interviews may be as short as 20 minutes or as long as two hours.

Meet the Candidates

Being interviewed alongside other candidates may be a daunting prospect for some, thus I have devised some guidelines and strategies that will carry you through and see you shine.

Friend or foe?

Whether fellow candidates are friends or foes matters not. The recruiters will be assessing your ability to positively interact with others so it is important to be friendly, considerate and respectful to everyone you meet.

Successful interaction

Successful interaction comes from understanding and respecting an individuals' personality. Read through the following personality guidelines to learn how to effectively interact with the varying types you are likely to encounter.

» The Aggressor
The aggressors that you will encounter in an interview environment are often covert and manipulative. They disguise their attacks as constructive criticism or harmless jokes so that, in the instance that they are confronted, they can deny any wrong doing. If you find yourself under attack from these predators, ask questions that will temp them into the open, such as: "That sounded like a disrespectful comment, was it?"

If the aggressor is more openly disrespectful and disparaging, the best approach is to remain calm and composed, listen attentively and without interruption until they have finished. A counter attack will only reflect badly on you so resist the tendency to fight back. Instead, acknowledge their opinion and then voice your own in a respectful manner.

» The Desperado
Some candidates will be in a position of sheer desperation for the job. Whether this is due to a real need or a simple desire, these individuals are likely to appear anxious and tense. Be friendly and empathetic with these candidates, but avoid getting drawn too deeply into conversation about of their hardship.

» The Model
In using the term 'model', I am not necessarily referring to looks. Rather, I am referring to those candidates who seem to be models of perfection. They appear to say and do all the right things, seemingly without a care or worry in the world. They naturally exude charisma and confidence, and have a magnetic personality.

In observing these candidates, examine what makes them appear perfect and then learn by their example. How do they stand? What do they do with their hands? How do they use their voice?

» The Overly Anxious
Some individuals become overwhelmed at interviews and will experience intense levels of stress, fear and panic. In this heightened state, the individual may experience uncontrollable symptoms such as blushing, stammering and shaking.

Experiencing a panic attack is very traumatic, so be friendly and supportive with these individuals. Offer words of encouragement, but don't place too much focus on their anxiety. Rather, try to break their state by asking questions about things they enjoy and that make them feel relaxed. You could ask them about their family, hobbies or desires.

» **The Extrovert**
Extroverts are very sociable creatures and thrive on interaction. They are comfortable speaking to large audiences, are very open with their thoughts and feelings, and take an enthusiastic approach to most activities.

As these extroverted types love to network, any time spent in discussion with them may be somewhat limited. While in their presence, enjoy the buzz they create and allow their enthusiasm to radiate through you.

If you have an introverted tendency, there may be a potential personality clash. Just bide your time and try to enjoy their vibrant presence.

» **The Actor**
Actors in this context refers to those candidates who put on an elaborate front to conceal their true personalities. These individuals are usually relatively harmless so, if you do happen to catch their act, it is probably best to not blow their cover.

If, however, it becomes obvious that this candidate has blatantly lied for the job, you may want to distance yourself to avoid being associated with their deceit.

» **The Know-It-All**
Know-it-alls have an attitude of superiority and like to think they are experts in everything. In conversation, they are arrogant and condescending and openly disregard the opinion of others. Some know-it-alls really are experts, so just agree with them and try to move on. If, however, the so called expert is not an expert at all, simply state the facts as you perceive them. Whatever you do, don't be drawn into a debate with either type because it will get messy.

» **The Dominator**
Can't get a word in? You may be encountering the dominator. In milder cases, dominators like to be the centre of attention and will talk incessantly to control the conversation. In extreme cases, they will be argumentative, rude and irrational.

In the face of a domineering person, remain calm and resist the natural urge to reason or retaliate. Instead, you should either try to distance yourself from the person, otherwise an assertive communication style is needed to push past this stickler. In this instance, remain calm, confident and respectful.

» **The Show-off**
You can be certain to find a show-off at every group interview. You will recognise him or her by their showy, self absorbed and obnoxious attitude. While this personality type is easily annoying, the truth is that these people tend to be deeply insecure. They brag about their own achievements through fear that nobody will otherwise notice. So, be kind and sincerely acknowledge their efforts when appropriate.

» **The Rival**
Naturally there will be candidates present who view you as competition and a threat to their success. Being competitive isn't a bad thing in itself unless these candidates put up barriers and become inwardly focused. In this instance, it is important to be friendly while respectful of their space. Remember, competitive people are passionate, driven and innovative, so embrace these positive traits.

» The Negativist
Ah, the negativist. There's always one in every crowd. At best, negativists are very annoying. At worst, they will drain every ounce of energy and motivation from your body. Attempts to motivate or encourage these people generally fall flat, so it's sometimes best not to say anything at all. So, remain positive and try to distance yourself as much as possible. If this is not possible, detach yourself from their words and stay focused on your own positive energy.

» The Leader
Natural leaders are instantly recognisable by their innate desire to step up. Their confident, assertive and intelligent character inspires trust in others while their sensitive, inspiring and sincere side inspires confidence. In the presence of a good leader, respect, support and encourage their efforts. Participate and be an active member of their team.

» The Gossiper
Some individuals like to point out other peoples flaws or failures in an attempt to feel superior. Beware of these gossiping individuals as you can be sure they will gossip about you too. In the first instance, attempt to change the subject. If they continue, discourage their behaviour directly by refusing to participate. If all fails, take your leave immediately.

» The Entertainer
Entertainers thrive on interaction. They are sociable, talkative and very energetic people and love to be the centre of attention. It is very easy to like the entertainer as they have a very down to earth and friendly attitude. When interacting with an entertainer, avoid being overly serious and just allow their positive energy to flow through you.

Meet the Recruitment Officers

Typically, there will be one to three official recruitment officers present during recruitment days. These officers may be HR personnel, or they may be working senior staff members. Either way, you can be sure that they are experienced recruitment professionals.

Successful interaction

To successfully interact with recruitment personnel, it is important to understand their styles and be prepared to deal with them accordingly. You will typically encounter two dominant styles of interviewer, I call these: The interrogation experts and the guardian angels.

» The interrogation expert
Interrogation experts believe that candidates will only show their true personalities while under intense pressure. As a result, they adopt a direct and intimidating style of questioning and will cross examine every answer you provide. During this onslaught of questioning, they will be observing your ability to remain calm and think on your feet. So, approach their questions in a calm and confident manner and be direct and succinct in your response.

» The guardian angel
Guardian angels believe that candidates are more open and natural when they feel relaxed. Thus, they will attempt to relieve the pressure of the atmosphere by engaging in friendly conversation. While their relaxed and friendly style can be a welcome relief, unsuspecting candidates may become overly casual and reveal more than is appropriate. Thus, caution is advised. The key is to be friendly yet professional, and never let your guard down.

Journal Notes

Group Activities

What Assessors Look For

Through your involvement and behaviour, assessors will be looking for evidence of key competencies and personality attributes that will enable you to work effectively within the role and cope with the demands of the job.

The six key competencies that will typically be assessed are:

» Communication skills
» Team spirit
» Interpersonal ability
» Leadership
» Customer focus
» Initiative

To determine these competencies, the assessors will be observing:

» Level of participation and interaction

» Behaviour towards the activities and your peers

» Communication and work style

» Ability to think on your feet and react to external pressure

» Ability to lead and willingness to follow

To make an effective evaluation, the recruiters will typically refer to a competency rating scale. This scale works on a points based system and the final result will reflect a candidates suitability for the position.

Competency Rating Scale

-1 Unacceptable	0 Needs Improvement	1 Effective	2 Proficient	3 Outstanding

3	Works effectively as a team member and builds strong relationships within it
0	Remains calm and confident, and responds logically and decisively in difficult situations
3	Understands other people's views and takes them into account
2	Contributes ideas and collaborates with the team
2	Takes a systematic approach to problem solving
3	Speaks with authority and confidence
3	Is thoughtful and tactful when dealing with people
-1	Is conscientious of completing tasks on time
3	Actively supports and encourages others
2	Participates as an active and contributing member of the team

Figure 11.   Competency Rating Scale Sample Form

Seven Heavenly Virtues

1. Have fun
   However silly or irrelevant the tasks may seem, your active involvement is essential. So, rather than concern yourself about external details, just relax and allow yourself to enjoy the process. This positive viewpoint will reflect well on your character, demonstrate enthusiasm, and make the experience a fun filled one for you.

2. Contribute
   Volunteering, contributing ideas and making suggestions is another great way to demonstrate your enthusiasm and team spirit. Furthermore, it will show that you are not afraid to take the initiative or express yourself and are keen to get involved.

3. Keep track of time
   If the recruiters set a time limit for any task, it is respectful to honour the deadline. Moreover, it will reflect positively on your listening skills, and demonstrate your attention to detail and ability to follow instructions. So, remain vigilant of the time and forewarn your peers when the deadline is approaching.

4. Summarise
   Summarising the main points of a discussion is a great way to move past awkward moments of silence and sticking points. The breathing room summarising creates will typically stimulate further ideas and encourage participation. Not only will your peers be grateful for the momentary relief, your communication and leadership ability will also be highlighted.

5. Use names
   Remembering people's names will demonstrate your ability to listen and pay attention to detail. Moreover, it will demonstrate a tremendous amount of respect for others and create a lasting impact.

6. Be positive
   When you choose to exhibit a positive spirit, people will naturally be drawn towards your character. So, be enthusiastic about the exercises you are asked to undertake and be encouraging towards others.

7. Encourage
   If any members of your team remain reserved, encourage their involvement by asking if they have an idea, suggestion or opinion. This shows empathy, consideration team spirit.

Seven Deadly Sins

1. Over involvement
   Getting involved and showing enthusiasm in a task is fantastic, but over involvement and incessant talking can leave others struggling to get involved and may transfer across to assessors as arrogance.

2. Under involvement
   For assessors to make an informed assessment, active involvement from each individual is essential. Those who are unable to get involved, for whatever reason, will surely be eliminated.

3. Disputing
   Conflicting views are natural, however, a group assessment is neither the time or place to engage in a hostile dispute with other candidates.

4. Criticising
   Even if your intentions are honourable and the feedback is constructive, criticising another candidates opinions, actions and ideas may be perceived as an attack.

5. Being negative
   Making negative remarks or exhibiting frustration over tasks, peers or previous employers , no matter how harmless it may seem, will raise serious concerns about your attitude and ethics.

6. Being bossy
   There is nothing wrong with striving for excellence, however, being dominant and imposing your ideas on others is overbearing and intimidating which leads others to feel incompetent.

7. Neglecting to listen
   Neglecting to listen to instructions leads to misinterpretations and displays a general lack of enthusiasm. Not listening or talking over others is ignorant and disrespectful.

Common Concerns

Being alienated

When there are a lot of different personalities in a group and the emotions are high, it can become difficult to get involved. This is especially true during a large group discussion. In these instances, you should employ some of the following strategies for getting your voice heard.

» Raise your hand
As simple as it seems, raising your hand will demand the attention of the group and let them know that you have something to say.

» Be assertive
If raising your hand reaps no results, you will have to be more assertive. Wait for a momentary pause in the conversation, and simple say "excuse me" before proceeding. This may feel uncomfortable for some of you, but it is imperative that you contribute. If done calmly and respectfully, the assessors will be impressed by your effort.

Dealing with anxiety

If you have read through and practised the techniques described on pages 31 through 45, you should not experience much difficulty in dealing with symptoms of anxiety.

For on the spot relief, the most effective techniques are:

» Subtle deep breathing (Page 41)

» Trigger positive anchors (Page 34)

» Silently repeat affirmations (Page 39)

» Change your focus (Page 39)

Whichever technique you use, don't allow it to distract your attention too much that you lose the flow of the discussion or task.

Handling disagreements

If you disagree with an approach being taken by the group or an idea which has been brought forth, it is perfectly reasonable to say so as long as you are constructive and positive in doing so.

Consider the following statements:

» Negative:
"That wouldn't work. I think we should…"

» Constructive:
"I see your point, Mark, but there are a number of issues that may arise with that approach. How about we consider…"

The former example attacks and ridicules the idea, while the latter demonstrates a positive acknowledgement before a new idea is introduced.

In the instance that your new idea is rejected, remain polite and seek input from the group. If you are clearly outnumbered, gracefully accept the decision and move on.

Being ridiculed

If your idea is ridiculed, resist the temptation to retaliate. Instead, remain cordial and respectful in your response. This graceful reaction will be duly noted and respected by the assessors.

Feeling uncertain

You don't always have to give an opinion when you speak. Supporting what someone else has said, asking a legitimate question, or commenting on an emerging theme are equally good ways to make your presence known without appearing as if you like the sound of your own voice.

Points to Consider

In most cases, the outcome of each task or topic is largely irrelevant. Assessors are more concerned with how well you perform in a team environment, how you communicate your ideas and interact with others, and what role you typically assume.

Thus, no matter how you feel, you should approach every task with a can do attitude and every topic in a calm and conversational tone.

Journal Notes

Practical Tasks

Bridging the Gap

Duration: 30 Minutes

Instructions

With the materials provided, design and construct a bridge which is strong enough to support a roll of sticky tape.

Materials

- » 5 sheets of A4 paper
- » A pair of scissors
- » 1 Metre length of sticky tape
- » 4 Drinking straws
- » 1 Metre length of string
- » 2 Elastic bands

Advertising Space

Duration: 40 Minutes

Instructions

ABC company has secured a prime time radio spot and needs a new commercial campaign.

Using the teams collective knowledge of the company, create a compelling commercial that will attract new customers.

The final broadcast must be no more than 45 seconds in length, and each team member must have an active role in the final presentation.

Points to Consider

This activity will highlight your knowledge of the company, so be ready with plenty of input from your research.

Who's Who?

Duration: 20 Minutes

Instructions

Pair off with a random partner and try to find out as much as you can about each other in twenty minutes.

When called upon, present your partner to the group.

Points to Consider

The purpose of this task is threefold.:

» How relevant is the information you gather?

» How confident are you when addressing a group?

» How well do you interact with new people.

Designer Wear

Duration: 45 Minutes

Instructions

ABC Company is looking to update its image and needs new designs for its staff uniform.

Consider the existing design and come up with a new or modified concept.

Points to Consider

During this task, be mindful of what is considered appropriate to the culture and industry.

Also, take inspiration from the current design as it provides valuable insight into what the company considers to be appropriate.

Journal Notes

Discussions

Shipwrecked

Duration: 45 Minutes

Instructions

Your plane has gone down over the Atlantic Ocean. There are eight survivors, but the one surviving life raft only has a capacity for four people.

As a team, identify four survivors from the following list who you would save and why. Select a spokesperson to present your decision and explain why you came up with the results.

Survivors

- » The pilot
- » A pregnant woman
- » An ex army general
- » A surgeon

- » The pope
- » A child
- » A nurse
- » An athlete

Points to Consider

Due to the very nature of this task, there is a potential for some strong emotions to be released. In such instances, remain calm and don't be tempted into a confrontation. Simply acknowledge and show respect for others opinions.

Survivor

Duration: 45 Minutes

Instructions

Your flight is scheduled to land in Los Angeles, however, due to mechanical difficulties the plane was forced to land on a remote island.

During landing, much of the equipment aboard was damaged, but 10 items have been recovered intact. Your task is to rank them in terms of their importance.

Items

- » A box of matches
- » 15 feet of nylon rope
- » 5 gallons of water
- » Signal flares
- » A self inflating life raft

- » A magnetic compass
- » First aid kit
- » A fruit basket
- » A tub of dry milk powder
- » A shotgun

Rags to Riches

Duration: 30 Minutes

Instructions

You have just won £1,000,000.00 on the lottery. From the five options below, which action would you take and why?

Options

- » Take early retirement
- » Give a large percentage to charity
- » Invest it into a business
- » Save it for your future
- » Spend it on luxuries

Day Trip

Duration: 30 Minutes

Instructions

You have been given the responsibility for arranging a day trip for 15 disabled children. Discuss where you would take the children, what activities you would have arranged and why.

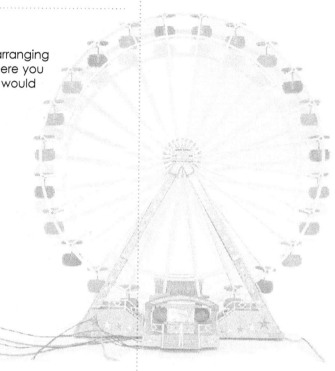

Options

» Theme park

» Museum

» White water rafting

» Trip on the Orient Express

» Water Park

» Safari

» Art gallery

» Scenic helicopter ride

Points to Consider

In this instance, the children in question are disabled. So, certain activities will not be appropriate, while others may not sufficiently capture the children's interest. It is important to gain a balance between having fun and being safe.

Role Play Scenarios

Role play scenarios may be performed with other candidates as a pair or within a group, or they may be performed one on one with an assessor.

The scenarios will bear some relation to the demands of the job and could include:

» Intoxicated customer

» Customer complaint

» Abusive behaviour

» Disorderly behaviour

The assessors don't expect you to know the answer to every possible scenario they introduce. They simply want to see how you react in challenging situations. So, when taking part in any role play scenario, use the following guidelines:

» Be proactive and do your best to resolve the situation using your initiative

» Remain calm and composed

» Be direct and assertive

» Immerse yourself into the role

» Take each scenario seriously

» Devise a plan and follow it as much as possible

Here are some pointers to help you deal with some common scenarios:

» Complaint
In the case of a customer complaint, it is important that you listen to their concern without interruption. Ask questions, where appropriate, to clarify their concerns and show empathy towards their situation. If the facts warrant it, apologise for the situation, explain what action you intend to take and thank them for bringing the matter to your attention.

» Intoxicated customer
Offer the customer a cup of tea or coffee and don't provide any more alcoholic drinks. You could also encourage the customer to eat some food. Remain calm towards the customer, but be direct and assertive in your approach. If you feel it appropriate, inform your senior and seek assistance from other staff members.

Journal Notes

Individual Assessments

Self Introduction

As well as learning more about you and your background, the self introduction is an opportunity for the recruiters to assess how well you cope when addressing a group of people and how articulately you are able to communicate your message. In their assessment, they will be looking for good delivery, and a certain amount of charisma.

To deliver a self introduction which makes an impact, here are some guidelines for you to consider.

» Make it relevant
  Use this opportunity to highlight your suitability for the job by sharing interesting facts about your present or most recent job, and your motives for making a career change.

  Consider the following example:
  " Hi everyone. My name is Jane and it's really nice to meet you all. I'm 27 years old and live in the bustling city of Bristol. I currently work as a freelance hair consultant, which is a job I really enjoy, but I have always wanted to be a beauty consultant which is why I am here today. Outside of work, I enjoy horse riding and am captain of the local football team"

» Be spontaneous
  A self presentation which is spontaneous will add life and sincerity to your speech. Sure you can prepare a rough draft and familiarise yourself with it, but don't try to learn it by heart as there is a risk of appearing forced, dull and monotone.

» Inject personality
  Show your passion and enthusiasm by injecting some emotion into your presentation.

» Be concise
  Unless advised otherwise, keep it relatively short and focused. Thirty to Sixty seconds should be sufficient.

» Rotate your focus
  To give the impression of confidence and engage your audience, rotate your gaze and make eye contact with various members for three to five seconds each.

» Adjust your voice
  Varying your tone, pitch, volume and pace will eliminate monotone and make it enjoyable for others to listen to. Slowing your pace slightly will also add clarity.

» Stick to the time limit
  If a time limit has been set, be sure to respect it.

Personality Questionnaire

Through a series of simple questions, personality tests provide assessors with an indication of a candidates character, behaviour and work style. The test results merely supplement the recruiters own observations from the interview and, as such, there are no right or wrong answers.

Typical questions you will encounter are:

For each question, give a mark out of five. One = Disagree strongly | Five = Agree strongly
» I enjoy meeting new people.
» I get bored with repetitive tasks.
» I often lose my temper when I am frustrated.
» I always think before I act.
» I work well under pressure.
» I find it easy to relax.
» I get on well with most people.
» I am a team player.
» I prefer to work alone.
» I become nervous in social situations.
» I find it difficult to communicate with other cultures.
» I thrive on challenges.

In an attempt to create a favourable impression, some candidates try to imagine how the recruiters want them to be and will answer questions dishonestly. I would advise against this strategy because any contradiction between your answers and the recruiters own observations will make it obvious that the answers have been embellished.

Numerical Ability Test

Depending on the industry, you may be required to undergo a numerical ability test. Numeracy tests are designed to test your basic arithmetic skills: Addition, subtraction, multiplication and division. While they are typically short and relatively simple in nature, if you haven't exercised your maths brain for some time, it may be a good idea to practice some basic mental arithmetic before the interview.

Here are some sample questions to get your juices flowing.

Tips for Success

When completing any kind of written test, it is important that you read the questions through fully and make sure you completely understand what is being asked before attempting to answer.

To be confident that you have answered as many questions as possible, it is always best to complete the questions you find easy on the first pass, returning to the trickier questions later.

To avoid handing in a form that is full of scribbles and mistakes, mark your answers out in pencil and carry out a final proof-read before you hand in your form.

Tips for Success

» Run through your times tables
» Practice some basic calculations like subtraction and multiplication
» Practice estimating answers without the use of a calculator
» Read each question and answer carefully - sometimes multiple choice answers are deliberately similar so take time to check each option. Pay particular attention to things like the unit of measurement or the number of decimal places.

Calculators may or may not be permitted.

1. What is Twelve Thousand Nine Hundred and Seventy Six in figures?
A. 129,76.00   B. 12,976,000   C. 12,976.00

2. What is 6 multiplied by 8?
A. 48   B. 52   C. 46

3. Add 67 to 12
A. 80   B. 79   C. 76

4. You begin with a float of 66.94. A customer purchases a pack of peanuts at 0.66, a shot of spirits at 3.54 and a pack of chewing gum at 0.53. How much float should you have following this transaction?
A. 62.21   B. 71.76   C. 71.67

5. There are 357 seats on your aircraft. The seats are divided into three cabins. How many seats are in each cabin?
A. 117   B. 119   C. 109

General Knowledge Quiz

General knowledge tests are fairly straightforward. The questions cover a broad range of topics and are likely to include political, geographical, historical, entertainment and scientific areas.
Here are some sample test questions to give you a better idea of what to expect.

» In relation to time, what does the abbreviation GMT stand for?
» How many continents are there?
» What is the name of the highest mountain in the world?
» Which is the largest continent?
» What is the capital of the USA?
» In which country would you find the river Nile?
» In which continent would you find Russia?
» Who is the president of the United States?
» Where will the next Olympics be held?

Formal Interview

What Assessors Look For

Within the formal interview, the recruiters will now seek to explore your motives for applying to their company and your desire for pursuing the position. Moreover, they will seek to gather information about your work history, character and work ethic to determine whether you will fit the job and company.

During the interview, they will examine your ability to listen actively, express yourself articulately, confidently and professionally, and answer questions logically and concisely. They will also be paying special attention to how you present yourself.

The Process

To ease you into the interview process and make you feel more open and relaxed, the recruiters will typically open the session with questions about you and your background.

They will then seek to explore your motivation for applying to the company and making a career change. Questions such as "Why do you want to work for us?" and "Why do you want to be a (...)?" are common at this stage.

With the interview thoroughly under way, the recruiters will want to determine whether you possess the skills and experience necessary for the position. Here you can expect more probing situational and behavioural questions, such as "When have you provided good customer service?" and "Describe a time when you failed to communicate effectively".

Duration

There appears to be no typical duration for formal interviews. Some of you will be in and out in as little as 20 minutes, while others may find the interview lasts for up to two hours.

Seven Heavenly Virtues

1. Stay focused
   If you fail to control your internal dialogue you will not only lose your composure, but you also risk misunderstanding the question. Remain completely focused on what the recruiter is saying and focus on giving the best possible answer. Concerns about how you look and the outcome should be postponed until after the interview.

2. Listen actively
   Although you should never interrupt the recruiter, you shouldn't listen in total silence either. Instead, use verbal feedback cues to indicate that you are listening and that you understand. This will encourage the recruiter to continue.

   Some verbal feedback signals include: "I see", "Yes", "I understand", "Sure".

3. Inject personality
   Injecting passion and personality into your answers will add life and sincerity. It will also keep the recruiters interested in what you are saying.

4. Be concise
   If an answer is too long-winded, the recruiter will become complacent. Keeping your answers short and concise will retain their attention.

5. Be positive
   A positive spirit will reflect well on your character and allow the recruiters to warm towards you. So, be enthusiastic about the interview and the job, and speak respectfully about your previous employers and positions.

6. Vary your voice
   Varying your tone, pitch, volume and pace will eliminate monotone and make it enjoyable for the recruiters to listen to. Slowing your pace slightly will also add clarity.

7. Maintain eye contact
   Regular, strong eye contact will give the impression of someone who is honest and confident.

   Where there is more than one recruitment officer, you should maintain eye contact with the person who asks you the question while occasionally engaging eye contact with the second recruiter .

Seven Deadly Sins

1. Controlling
   Trying to lead or control the conversation will appear arrogant and disrespectful. Ask questions when appropriate opportunities arise, but allow the recruiter to do his or her job.

2. Interrupting
   Interruptions are rude and disrespectful to the speaker. So, unless absolutely necessary, you should allow the recruiter to finish speaking before responding or asking for clarification.

3. Lying
   If you lie, there will be a very good chance that you will be caught out when the recruiters probe into your answers with follow up questions. If this happens, you could end up looking rather silly and, worse still, any chance of being offered the job will be ruined.

4. Being negative
   Making negative remarks or exhibiting frustration over tasks, peers, other company's or previous employers, no matter how harmless it may seem, will raise serious concerns about your attitude and ethics.

5. Unprepared or unnecessary questions
   To stand out as an informed and competent applicant, your questions should reflect that you have researched the company and the position. Asking questions that have already been addressed within the company's literature will make you appear unprepared and incompetent.

   Likewise, asking questions that are based on money and benefits will make you appear selfishly motivated and give a negative impression about your motives for the position and/or the company.

6. Talking incessantly
   It's easy to talk too much when nervous, however, it is important to remember that interviews are two-way exchanges. A moment of silence, while it might seem awkward to you, lets the recruiter know that you are done and allows them to move the interview along.

7. Overusing filler words
   The useless and annoying verbal mannerisms "you know," "like," "in other words," "kind of," "ummm," and "anyways." should be avoided at all costs. Besides making you sound unprofessional, they also detract attention from your message.

Journal Notes

Surviving the Q&A

Competency Based Questions
Traditional Questions
Interviewing the Interviewer

Competency Based Questions

Introduction

The theory behind competency-based interview questions (also known as behavioural or situational questions) lies in the belief that how you have behaved and applied certain skills in the past will determine how you will behave in the future. Thus, recruiters use this style of questioning to predict applicants' future performance as well as to determine whether an applicant possesses the particular qualities, skills and experiences required for the job.

Preparing Examples

The key to preparing for competency-based questions is to study the job description and person specification. With this information, you can identify the core competencies that are required and prepare examples that demonstrate those competencies.

Company's recruiting for customer facing positions will certainly be looking for candidates who demonstrate:

- » Communication competence
- » Interpersonal ability
- » Customer focus
- » Team spirit
- » Leadership
- » Initiative

When preparing your examples, don't overlook those of a difficult or negative nature as you will surely be asked to illustrate some of these. To say that you haven't faced any difficulties would sound dishonest and naive.

Before you plunge in, however, you need to be very selective in your choices. For instance, it would be unwise to volunteer a negative example that involves a core skill, or one which had an undesirable impact on the company, colleagues or customers.

The most effective answer in this instance is one that shows that you understand that mistakes are occasionally part of the professional growth process, and that you are able to remain calm and learn from these experiences.

The S.A.R.R Formula

S.A.R.R is an acronym for Situation - Action - Result - Reflection

When preparing your examples, the S.A.R.R formula can help you structure your response.

» Situation
  Begin by briefly describing the challenge, problem, or task.

» Action
  Go on to describe what you did, how and why you did it.

» Result
  Describe the outcome and how your actions affected the outcome or the people involved

» Reflection
  Finally, you may offer a reflection. This can include what you learned from the experience and whether you would do anything differently in the future.

Consider the following example:

» Situation:
  "I was in the staff room during my lunch break, and I could hear a lot of noise coming from inside the salon. I went to investigate and I was confronted by two, very bored, little girls. I could sense that their excitement was causing a disruption and inconvenience"

» Action:
  "I immediately took the initiative and attempted to occupy them by offering to plait their hair while they made bracelets from some hair beads. Their eyes sparkled with excitement and I was able to keep them occupied for the remainder of their visit"

» Result:
  "We had lots of fun and, while the calm was restored, the stylist was able to complete the clients' treatment"

» Reflection:
  "I felt really pleased that with just a little extra effort, I had made such a big difference"

Follow up Questions

Although the S.A.R.R formula will eliminate the recruiters need to ask some follow up questions, there will always be areas that the recruiter wants to probe further into. So, it is important to have examples ready to back up any statements made.

Prepare to be asked:

» What did you learn from the experience?

» What specifically did you say?

» How did you feel?

» Would you do anything differently?

» How did they react?

» What other options did you consider?

» Why did you decide to take the action that you did?

» You mentioned ... Tell me more about that.

» How did you retain your composure?

» Can you give me an example of that?

» Can you be more specific about ...?

In some circumstances, the recruiter may even interrupt your responses with supplementary questions. Take a look at the following example.

» Candidate
"Working in a creative environment with other highly skilled professionals, it was natural that we had the occasional clash of ideas."

» Recruiter
"Please can you elaborate further?"

» Candidate
"We would sometimes have a clash of ideas based around our individual preference towards certain products, styles, magazines or equipment. Although, any disagreements we did have were relatively minor and insignificant."

» Recruiter
"What would you consider minor and insignificant?"

» Candidate
"Our debates were never confrontational, and they never interfered with our work in any way. In fact, some disagreements were quite educational."

» Recruiter
"Educational?"

» Candidate
"Yes, some very interesting views emerged from these debates which sometimes resulted in people, including myself, having a slight change in perspective."

» Recruiter
"Can you tell me about a change you had in perspective following such a debate?"

....

Lack of relative experience

If you don't have any relative experience in a particular area, you need to be honest and say so, but don't just leave it there. Use the opportunity to remind the recruiters of the skills that you do have or explain how you would handle the situation if it arose.

If you have faced a similar situation, you could say "I can't remember ever being in that situation, however, I did face something slightly similar that I could tell you about?".

Sample
Answers

1   When have you gone out of your way for a customer?

Sample Response 1

Situation:
I had a client call into the store who was looking for a very specific style of fabric. She had visited several stores in and around the area but hadn't been successful in her search.

I could see that she was exhausted, but also very determined. She spoke with such sorrow in her voice that I actually began to feel sorry for the poor lady because I didn't have the fabric to sell her.

Action:
Not wanting to be the bearer of more bad news, I decided to offer my assistance. I spent several hours ringing around wholesalers, distributors and manufacturers trying to track down this particular fabric, when finally I struck gold with a small manufacturing plant.

Result:
Because the fabric was a special order, there was a small handling charge, but the customer received the fabric within a few days and was sure it was worth the expense and wait.

Sample Response 2

Situation:
I encountered a problem when one of my clients was unable to have a hair treatment carried out in her home because it was being renovated.

Action:
In an attempt to keep the client, I spoke to a contact I had within a local salon and was able to negotiate a small fee for use of the salon facilities.

Result:
This worked out really well because it was convenient for both myself and the client to travel to. Since then, I have negotiated similar deals with four other salons and have increased my customer base dramatically as a direct result.

2 Describe a time when your customer service could have been better?

Evaluation

Providing excellent customer service is vital, so you should be very cautious when providing negative examples.

You could take a modest approach and explain that you always strive to do better, or you could be honest with humble example.

Alternatively, you could attempt to avoid providing an example by explaining how you maintain your standards, and then proceed with an example of a time when you have demonstrated this capability.

Sample Response (Modest approach)

I take great pride in providing the best service I possibly can, but in doing so I increase my skills and can always see room for improvement.

Sample Response (No experience)

I take great pride in providing the best service I possibly can, and I never let my standards slip. Even during times of high pressure, I make an effort to remain courteous and helpful. I can honestly say that I have never received any negative feedback.

3 | When have you solved a customer problem?

Evaluation

The recruiter wants to get an idea of how you apply your initiative and problem-solving skills to customer related issues. A good answer here will demonstrate that you always put in extra effort to provide good customer service and are not intimidated by difficult situations.

Sample Response

Situation:
I remember a client who came to me to have her hair extensions replaced. She had worn sewn in extensions for several months and was experiencing some discomfort from the attachments.

Action:
As I examined her hair, I was shocked to discover how much damage had been caused. Her roots had become severely matted and the tightness from the installed tracks had created spots of baldness.

I took a moment to analyse the situation, work out a strategy and then I set to work.

I spent several hours meticulously untangling every hair and removing every extension piece, The more I removed, the more I could see the scale of the damage that had been caused. Sadly, the client's hair was in very bad shape after the removal and the spots of baldness were very evident. Needless to say, I had a very emotional customer.

I applied a very deep conditioning protein treatment to the customers remaining locks and gave it a good trim. I then finished up with some fine and strategically placed fusion hair extensions to conceal the bald patches and create some much needed volume.

Result:
Following the treatment, the client looked fantastic and her smile was restored. Her hair soon returned to its former glory and she became a regular client of mine.

4 · When have you tended to an upset customer?

Evaluation

The recruiter is trying to grasp your ability to cope with stressful situations. A good answer will suggest that you can think on your feet, and display a positive and patient attitude when challenging situations arise.

Sample Response

Situation:
I recently experienced a situation with a client who was having relationship problems. She was becoming increasingly emotional and I could sense that she was feeling very depressed.

Action:
Although I felt compassion for her situation, I knew that it was important for me not to get overly involved. So, I gave her chance to talk while I listened, and I tried to show empathy while remaining neutral and professional in my response.

Result:
Just being able to talk to someone who listened seemed to make her feel better. As she continued to speak, she appeared to have gained a deeper insight into her situation and actually began seeing things more positively. Consequently, she was able to calmly discuss her feelings with her partner and work through their problems. She later thanked me for listening.

Reflection:
From this experience, I learned that just listening can be providing good customer care.

5 Have you been confronted by an aggressive customer?

Evaluation

The ability to remain well-mannered and well-tempered while dealing with an aggressive customer is an absolute necessity. The recruiter will want to assess whether you can deal with confrontational issues in a calm and rational manner.

You will be assessed on how well you coped under the pressure and how you dealt with the customer. A good response will show that you never lost your temper and remained courteous throughout the experience.

Sample Response

Situation:
Shortly after I began freelancing, I encountered a problem when an associate of mine tried to pressure me into a free service based on friendship.

Action:
I proceeded to offer her, what I considered to be, a reasonable discount, but she was not satisfied with my offer and proceeded to pressure me with emotional blackmail. I remained cordial, but became more assertive as I continued to refuse her demands.

Result:
Rather than accept the reasons for my decision, she became increasingly enraged, and even began to slander my service and friendship

Shocked at her over-reaction, and concerned about what might develop, I felt I had no option but to withdraw from the situation.

Reflection:
This experience was very challenging and certainly tested my patience. But I remained calm and, although this particular relationship never recovered, it was a learning experience that hasn't since been repeated.

6 When have you had to say 'No' to a customer?

Evaluation

There will be occasions when it is necessary to say no to a customer. The recruiter wants to know that you aren't intimidated by such situations and have the strength of character to deal with the situation authoritatively, yet diplomatically.

You will be assessed on how you approached the customer and went about dealing with the situation. A good response will demonstrate your ability to use tact, and will show that you remained courteous throughout the experience.

Sample Response

Situation:
I remember when a customer tried to return a pair of trainers to the store for a refund. Although the customer denied it, I could see that the shoes had clearly been worn.

Action:
I remained calm and polite as I suggested that the shoes could not be returned unless faulty or unused.

The customer become very aggressive and repeatedly threatened to contact our head office to complain about me if I didn't refund him immediately.

I remained assertive and suggested this would be the best course of action for him to take. I then proceeded to provide him with the full details of our complaints manager within the head office.

Result:
Realising defeat, the man stormed out of the shop and, to my knowledge, never did take the matter further.

7 | When have you handled a customer complaint?

Sample Response

Situation:
I remember when a customer complained about a meal they had purchased.

Because over two thirds of the entire course had been eaten, not only was it obvious that the complaint was insincere, but it was also against the restaurants policy to offer a refund under such circumstances.

The customer was becoming very enraged and threatened to write to the trading standards and newspapers if I did not give him a full refund.

Action:
I gave the customer my undivided attention while he vented his frustrations. Then, when he had finally calmed down, I calmly apologised for the dissatisfaction and proceeded to offer a meal deal voucher as a goodwill gesture.

Result:
The customer was clearly unhappy not to have received a refund, but he left the restaurant and, as suspected, never did take the matter any further.

8

When have you had to resolve a conflict between what the customer wanted and what you could realistically deliver?

Evaluation

The recruiter wants to determine that you have the strength of character to voice your concerns. They also want to see that you can be diplomatic, yet authoritative, in your communication style.

You will be assessed on how you approached the customer and how you dealt with the situation.

Sample Response

Situation:
I remember a client who came to me for a colour treatment and restyle. She had used a virtual hairstyle software to create her ideal look and was beaming with excitement as she showed me the picture.

The style was notably very pretty, and it was clear that it was ideally suited to the client. Unfortunately, however, the client's hair had been through several perming and colour treatments, and the platinum blonde shade that she wanted just wasn't going to be possible at that time.

Action:
Knowing how excited the client was, I felt a little dejected as I proceeded to break this news to her. In the hope of relieving some of her obvious disappointment, I suggested a strand test to see if it would be possible to lift some of the colour without causing excessive damage. If the strand test were a success, we could perform a gradual transformation through the use of highlights.

Result:
Thankfully, the strand test was a success and the client, while naturally disappointed, was happy to go ahead with the gradual transformation. The result was striking,and the client was happy with the result.

Within nine months, the transformation was complete, and I had a very satisfied customer.

9 | Describe a situation when the customer was wrong

Evaluation

Although the popular saying suggests otherwise, the customer isn't always right and the recruiter wants to know that you aren't Intimidated by such situations.

You will be assessed on how you approached the customer and went about dealing the situation. A good response will demonstrate your ability to use tact, and will show that you remained courteous throughout the experience.

Sample Response

Situation:
I remember a client who I had carried out a perming treatment for. After completing the treatment, I provided written instructions for how to care for her new perm which specifically instructed against washing the hair for at least 48 hours.

Unfortunately, the very next day the client washed her hair and the perm dropped out. The client was understandably very upset, but refused to accept that the perm had fallen out as a consequence of her own actions. She became very irate and started to slander my work and the salon.

Action:
When asked if she had followed the instructions, she denied being provided with any. I assured her that instructions were provided, and suggested she check her belongings.

Result:
Later that afternoon, the client returned to the salon holding onto the instruction sheet with a very embarrassed look on her face. She apologised profusely for her behaviour.

Reflection:
To avoid a repeat of this situation, I now provide clearer warnings within the written information sheet and back it up with verbal instructions.

10 Have you ever bent the rules for a customer?

Evaluation

There are situations where it is permissible to bend the rules, however, some company's may view rule bending very negatively. So, no matter how trivial or well-intended, you may want to play it safe and declare that you have never gone against the rules.

If you do decide to provide an answer, you should show that you are able to keep balance between company policy and the interest of customers.

Sample Response

I have always abided by company policies and have never bent the rules. Bending the rules for one customer, will no doubt lead to a downward spiral . Either the customer will expect further rule bending, or other customers will catch on and expect the same treatment. It's just not a wise course of action to take.

11 Tell me about a time when you failed to communicate effectively?

Evaluation

We all experience challenges in communication, but a complete failure to communicate effectively will show a lack of initiative and creativity in problem solving.

Whatever the reason for a communication challenge, there is always a way to communicate if you are willing to put in some additional effort. Your answer should reflect this.

Sample Response (Modest Approach)

While I have certainly encountered communication challenges, I can honestly say that I have never yet completely failed in my ability to communicate. With some creativity, I have always found a way to overcome communication barriers.

Sample Response (Humble Example)

Situation:
Generally, I am a very efficient communicator, but I do recall when I experienced difficulty communicating with an OAP client.

Action:
The client was very hard of hearing, and I tried everything to communicate with her. I spoke slower, louder, used hand gestures and facial expressions, I even tried to write the information down, but without her glasses she was unable see my writing clearly.

Result:
Fortunately, I managed to locate a magnifying glass, which enabled the client to read my instructions, and everything worked out well in the end.

12

When have your communication skills made a difference to a situation or outcome?

Evaluation

The ability to communicate well is vital to customer facing roles, so you should have plenty of real life examples ready to share. This is your chance to shine, so don't be modest.

Sample Response

Situation:
I remember a trainee apprentice we had in our department who never asked questions and refused all offers of help. Unfortunately, instead of trying to understand her reasons, everyone drew the conclusion that she was a know-it-all and vowed not to offer help in the future.

Action:
Concerned that her progress would suffer, I decided to offer my encouragement and support. It soon became evident from our conversation that she had excessively high expectations of herself and feared looking incompetent. I explained that it was okay to ask questions, and mistakes were expected. I even shared a few of my own early mishaps to lighten the mood.

Result:
Very quickly after that we saw a change in her behaviour. She began asking questions, she was more open to suggestions, and her skills improved immensely.

Reflection:
From this experience, I learnt that things are not always what they appear and we need to be more objective before making rash judgements.

13

Give an example of when you had to present complex information in a simplified manner in order to explain it to others

Evaluation

In certain industries, you may be required to break down and convey complex information to customers. Your answer here should show that you are able to express knowledge in a clear and simple manner.

Sample Response

Situation:
I remember a client who was interested in having a colour treatment carried out. She was very inquisitive and asked numerous questions, so I could sense that she was concerned about the process and potential damage to her natural hair.

Action:
Not satisfied with a simple nontechnical version, I had to provide a detailed technical breakdown of the whole process. This involved describing the molecular structure of the hair, the effect colour particles have and how they bond to the structure.

Result:
Although I had to occasionally refer to training manuals to emphasise or clarify my point, overall the client was satisfied with my effort. As a direct result, she went ahead with the treatment and was very pleased with the outcome.

14 | Have you ever had to overcome a language barrier?

Evaluation

In today's multicultural societies, the ability to relate to others and adapt your communication style is very important.

Sample Response

Situation:
During a trip to Africa, I became acquainted with a French lady. She understood my French, the little amount I knew, but she didn't really understand English. Unfortunately, the amount of French I knew wasn't enough to get me through a whole conversation, so I had to improvise.

Action:
I spoke French wherever possible and filled in the gaps with improvised sign language and facial expressions.

Result:
At first it was a little tricky trying to find imaginative ways to communicate, but over time I became much more proficient. I'm sure she was amused by my amateur efforts, but it worked out well and I came away with a new friend.

Reflection:
Now when I encounter this type of communication barrier, I am much more confident in my ability to cope.

15 Tell me about a time that you had to work as part of a team

Sample Response

Situation:
There was a particular time that stands out for me because it was such an unusual occurrence.

It was a usual quiet Tuesday afternoon and only myself, the senior stylist, an apprentice, and the salon manager were on duty. To our surprise, it was as if someone started offering out free chocolate, as clients started to filter through the doors.

Action:
Despite the overwhelming rush, we showed great teamwork as we pulled together and shared our duties. Even our manager showed great team spirit as she got involved with the hair service.

Result:
As a result of our teamwork, and some free relaxing conditioning treatments, we managed to deliver an outstanding service. Every client went away completely satisfied.

16 When have you struggled to fit in?

Sample Response

Situation:
When I started working at Trina's Hair & Beauty, I was joining a very close-knit team who had been together for a number of years.

As a result of the number of trainees they had witnessed come and go over the years, they had become a little reluctant to accept new trainees.

I wouldn't say it was a struggle to fit in as such, but I certainly experienced some growing pains. With remarks such as 'if you are still here then' to contend with, I knew I had to prove myself.

Action:
To show that I was serious about the job, and was not a fly-by-night, I focused a lot of effort on learning my new job. At the same time, I continued to be friendly and respectful of my new colleagues while I made a conscious effort to get to know them.

Result:
As a result of my hard effort, It didn't take long for them to accept me and include me as part of their team. Naturally, I have become closer to some of my colleagues than with others, but we all got on and worked well as a team.

17 Have you ever experienced difficulties getting along with colleagues?

Evaluation

No matter how hard we try, or how likeable we are, there will always be someone that we don't hit it off with. To say otherwise, would not sound credible.

For the most part, this question is asked to determine your ability to get along with other people and manage adversity. The recruiters want to know that you don't allow conflict to interfere with work.

The best answer should show that you aren't intimidated or confrontational in such situations, but you put in the commitment necessary to build a respectful and healthy working relationship.

Sample Response

Situation:
I remember one co-worker in particular who flat out didn't like me. It didn't matter what I did or said, or whether I tried to avoid or befriend this person.

Action:
After a couple of days of subtle hostility, I decided to assert myself. I diplomatically explained that I acknowledged her dislike for me and I asked for input as to what I must do to create a professional relationship

Result:
Although we never became friends, we were able to maintain more cordial relations thereafter.

18 Tell us about a challenge you have faced with a colleague

Evaluation

It is almost guaranteed that you will encounter challenging situations with colleagues.

The recruiters want to know that you aren't intimidated by such colleagues or situations, and are prepared to use your initiative to diffuse or mediate as necessary to keep working relationships healthy.

Your answer should demonstrate your willingness to cooperate with others to resolve differences, improve relations, and manage conflicts. It should also display your ability to remain patient and positive in the face of adversity.

Sample Response

Situation:
I do remember one situation where two of my colleagues really didn't hit it off with one another. They were constantly quarrelling and everyone had lost patience with them, but no one wanted to get involved.

Action:
In the end, I decided to take the initiative and act as a sort of mediator to the situation. I was not their manager, so I had to be as tactful as I could so that I wouldn't upset anyone.

I started by explaining that I acknowledged their dislike for each other and then I drew upon the fact that they are both professionals and can, therefore, put aside their differences for the good of the team.

Result:
They had a pretty frank discussion and, although I can't say they ended up the best of friends, they did work out an effective strategy for working more productively together.

19 | Tell me about a disagreement with a colleague

Evaluation

We all have disagreements with colleagues, but they should never get out of control or interfere with work.

You may choose to disclose the details of a conflict situation, but make sure it was minor and didn't interfere with work. Conversely, you may wish to play it safe and declare that while you have had disagreements, they were so minor that you don't really recall the exact details. You could then go on to reiterate some minor examples.

The recruiters want to know that you aren't intimidated by conflicts and have the ability to see things from another person's perspective. Your answer should demonstrate that you are prepared to use your initiative and interpersonal skills to improve relations with colleagues, even in cases where they cannot agree upon certain issues.

Sample Response

Introduction:
Working in a creative environment with other highly skilled professionals, it was natural that we had the occassional clash of ideas. Any disagreements we did have, however, were so relatively minor and insignificant that I would be hard pressed to recall the exact details.

Situation:
Our disagreements were usually as a result of our individual preference towards certain products, styles, magazines or equipment.

Action:
Our debates were never confrontational and they never interfered with our work in any way.

Result:
In fact, some very interesting views emerged from these debates which sometimes resulted in people, including myself, having a slight change in my perspective. So, they were often very educational.

20 Have you successfully worked with a difficult coworker?

Sample Response

Situation:
I remember one member of staff was always complaining. Nothing was ever good enough or couldn't possibly work. Everyone had lost patience with her but, because she was so incredibly sensitive, no one said anything.

Action:
I spent some time with her and tactfully told her that it appeared as if she was always putting our ideas down.

Result:
On hearing this feedback she was genuinely horrified at her own behaviour. She explained that she hadn't realised it had made everyone feel that way and agreed that from then on she would try to be more positive.

Very quickly after that we saw a change in her behaviour. She became more conscious of her own attitude and deliberately tried to be more considerate. From that point on, no one could have hoped for a more committed team member.

21 | Have you ever worked with someone you disliked?

Evaluation

There will always be someone that we don't like and to try to convince the recruiter otherwise would not sound honest or credible.

For the most part, this question is asked to determine your ability to get along with other people and manage adversity. The recruiters want to know that you don't allow personal views cause conflict or interfere with work.

The best answer should show that you aren't intimidated or confrontational in such situations, but you put in the commitment necessary to build a respectful and healthy working relationship

Sample Response

Situation:
There was one colleague I worked with that I really found it difficult to get along with personally.

Action:
Instead of focusing on those things I didn't like, I put my personal views aside and focused on the skills she brought to the position.

Result:
My personal view of her never changed, and we never became friends, but we did work productively alongside each other without any problems.

22 Have you ever acted as a mentor to a coworker?

Evaluation

There may be times when you have to mentor new staff members and the recruiters are trying to assess your ability to lead and mentor your colleagues.

Sample Response

Situation:
I remember when one of our trainees was having problems understanding certain aspects of her course material, and I could see she was becoming increasingly frustrated and self critical.

Action:
Having witnessed her in action, I knew that she was a very bright and talented individual with no obvious lack of skill. So, I determined that her frustrations were probably the result of the pressure she was feeling about her approaching exam.

Concerned at the effect this pressure was having on her, and having experienced the same pressures myself, I decided to offer my support. To reinforce her understanding, I demonstrated some of the techniques she had been struggling with and showed her a few memory tips and tricks which had helped me through my exams.

Result:
My breakdown of the processes, along with the visual demonstration I provided, seemed to make the material much more understandable for her. In the days that followed, she seemed to have a new lease of life and was much more positive. Subsequently, she passed her exams with top grades.

23

What have you done that shows initiative?

Sample Response

Situation:
When I began working for my current employer, the inventory system was outdated and the storage room was very messy and disorganised.

Action:
I came in on my day off, cleaned up the mess, organised the store cupboards and catalogued it all on the new inventory forms.

Result:
Thereafter, when orders arrived it was easy to organise and retrieve.

Reflection:
If I'm able to do the task, instead of waiting for the job to be done, I simply do it.

24 Have you undertaken a course of study, on your own initiative, in order to improve your work performance?

Evaluation

Your answer here should show that you are committed to self-development and take the initiative when it comes to improving yourself and your efficiency.

Sample Response

Situation:
While at Trina's Hair Salon, we were experiencing a spectacular rise in demand for high fashion cuts. I had some creative cutting experience, but nothing that extended to the kind of advanced skill that was required for true high fashion cuts.

Action:
After some consideration, I decided that increasing my creative cutting skills would not only give the salon a competitive advantage, but it would also be a fantastic opportunity for me to move my skills to the next level. So, I took the initiative and, under my own funding, immediately enrolled onto a creative cutting course.

Result:
My new skills proved to be an instant success. Existing clients began recommending me to their friends, which resulted in a massive rise in clientele. Needless to say, my manager was very happy.

25 Describe an improvement that you personally initiated

Sample Response

Situation:
While travelling in India, I learnt the art of Indian head massage.

Action:
When I returned to work, I began using my new skill on clients while carrying out the shampoo.

Result:
My massages were becoming such a success, that my manager approached me to request that I train my colleagues. Naturally, I was honoured to oblige.

26 Describe a new idea or suggestion that you made to your supervisor

Evaluation
The recruiter wants to know that you aren't afraid to take the initiative and suggest improvements.

Sample Response

Situation:
When I was working at Trina's Hair Salon, I had noticed that a lot of our clients wore nail extensions.

Action:
Convinced that the service would be an improvement to our already successful salon, I carried out extensive independent research before presenting the idea to my manager.

Result:
After carrying out her own research, she liked the idea so much that she decided to go ahead with the new service. Within a couple of months, the service was up and running, and we experienced a dramatic increase in new clientele and revenue. I even got a small bonus in my pay packet for my involvement.

27 Tell me about a problem you encountered and the steps you took to overcome it

Evaluation

The recruiter will be assessing how well you cope with diverse situations, and how you use your judgment and initiative to solve problems.

In answering this question, you need to provide a concrete example of a problem you faced, and then Itemize the steps you took to solve the problem. Your answer should demonstrate a patient and positive attitude towards problem solving.

Sample Response

Situation:
Early in my freelancing career, I experienced several clients who turned up late to their appointments. Some even forgot about their appointments altogether. Rather than just simply being an inconvenience, it was wasting my time and money.

Action:
I considered my options and decided that the best solution would be to send out reminder cards a few days prior to client appointments. For the repeat offenders, I would enforce a late cancellation fee.

Result:
This decision drastically cut the number of late arrivers, and I have never since had a no-show.

28 Tell me about a problem that didn't work out

Evaluation

No matter how hard we try, there are some instances where a problem just doesn't work out. To say otherwise will not sound honest or credible.

In answering this question, you need to first ensure that the problem was a minor one which had no negative or lasting impact on the company, a colleague or a customer. Try to accentuate the positives and keep your answer specific. Itemize the steps you took to deal with the problem and make it clear that you learnt from the experience.

Sample Response

Situation:
Shortly after I began freelancing, my bank returned a client's cheque to me through lack of funds.

Action:
At first, I was sure it was a mistake caused through an oversight on the part of my client. I made a number of calls, left several messages and even attempted a visit to the clients home, all to no avail.

Several weeks passed and it was clear that I was chasing a lost cause. At this point, I had to decide whether to write off the debt and blacklist the client or visit the Citizens' Advice for advice on retrieving the funds.

Result:
After careful consideration of all the factors involved, I decided to write the debt off as a learning experience.

Reflection:
In hindsight, I realise it was a silly mistake that could easily have been avoided. I have never repeated this error since as I now wait for the funds to clear before carrying out a service.

29 Have you ever taken the initiative to solve a problem that was above your responsibilities?

Sample Response

Situation:
It had been quite an uneventful afternoon when, all of the sudden, in walked an obviously frantic customer.

From what I could understand, her laptop had contracted a virus while connected to the internet and the system now failed to respond to any commands.

Being a self-employed web designer, the customer was naturally very concerned about the potential loss of data, and earnings.

Unfortunately, while the laptop was still within warranty, it was beyond the companies scope and had to be sent to the manufacturer for restoration. My colleagues, while polite, but could only offer assistance as far as sending the laptop to the manufacturer.

Action:
I could sense the customer was becoming increasingly distressed and, having had previous training in system restoration, I was confident that I could at least safely extract the data from the hard drive.

After talking the customer through the procedure, she granted her permission and I proceeded.

Result:
After some 45 minutes of fiddling with wires and hard drives, the customer's data had been successfully, and safely, extracted. The customer gasped a big sigh of relief as we packaged the laptop off to the manufacturer for repair.

Several weeks later, my line manager received a letter from the customer complimenting my efforts.

Reflection:
I was really pleased that a little effort made such a big difference.

30 | When have you made a bad decision?

Evaluation

We all make decisions that we regret, and to say otherwise will not sound honest or credible.

The recruiter will be assessing whether you have the character to admit and take responsibility for your mistake, whether your decision had a negative impact on customers or the company, and whether you learnt from this mistake?

In answering this question, you need to first ensure that the mistake was a minor one, which had no negative or lasting impact on the company, a colleague or a customer. Try to accentuate the positives and keep your answer specific. Itemize what you did and how you did it. Finally, you need to make it clear that you leant from the mistake and will be certain not to repeat it.

Sample Response

Situation:
Early in my freelance career, I was approached by a salesman who was promoting a protein conditioning system. He described the system as "The newest technology to emerge from years of research. Guaranteed to help heal, strengthen, and protect".

Although I was excited by the concept, I did have my concerns that the system sounded too good to be true. However, the salesman had all the official paperwork to back up his claims, and the literature was thorough and well presented. All these things, combined with the company's full money-back guarantee, made it appear to be a win-win situation, and a risk worth taking. So I invested.

Following my investment, I decided to test the system out on training heads before taking the system public. Unfortunately, several months of using the system passed with no obvious benefits.

Action:
Disappointed with the product, I decided to pursue the full money back guarantee, but the sales number was not recognised, and my letters were returned unopened. Even their website had mysteriously vanished. I soon came to the realisation that I had been taken in by an elaborate scam.

I contacted the Citizens Advice Bureau and Trading Standards, but there was little they could do to retrieve my funds.

Result:
Unfortunately, I never recovered my costs and had to put the mistake down to a learning experience.

Reflection:
Unfortunately, it really was my fault. I should have trusted my gut instinct and carried out thorough research before making my decision. It is a mistake I shall never repeat.

31 | What was the biggest challenge you have faced?

Sample Response

Situation:
To be honest, giving up smoking was the biggest challenge. I never thought I could do it, and I had made dozens of attempts that ended in failure.

Action:
Determined not to give in to my withdrawals, I decided I needed an incentive that would pull me through the tough times. Being sponsored for a worthy cause was the perfect solution.

Result:
With a good cause in mind, the following three months were easier than on previous occasions. Not only have I come out the other end a non-smoker, I also managed to raise £2464.00 for Childline.

Reflection:
Since I gave up smoking, I have gained so much personal insight, and I deal with potentially stressful situations at work so much more effectively now, I feel more energetic, more mentally alert and far calmer now than I ever did before.

Traditional Questions

Tell me about yourself

"As you can see from my résumé, I currently work as a (...), and have worked in client-facing roles for the past eight years. During this time, I have worked my way up from a (...) to a (...), while simultaneously studying for my (...).

Now, this brings me to why I am here today, interviewing with you.

I have always wanted to become a (...) and, during the course of my career, I have been gradually mastering the skills needed to perform its tasks. I'm confident that the customer care and teamwork skills I have developed throughout the course of my career, combined with my friendly and positive nature, will complement your existing team and enable me to deliver the standard of service that customers have come to expect from ABC Company.

I'd now like to discuss how I might continue my success by joining your team."

Reveal your passion

An honest and passionate response to this question will surely set you apart. Think about it, why do you really want the job? Where did the desire come from? Was it a childhood dream, or was it sparked by another interest?

Why do you want to become a (...)?

"As a child, I was fascinated by (...). This is where my passion for (...) initially began, but it wasn't until I carried out a career suitability test at college that I really started to consider (...) as a serious future prospect. The test examined personal attributes, interests and skills, and the final result came back suggesting suitability for the occupation. I done some further research into the job and instantly agreed. This job is tailored to my personality, skills and experience and is one I will feel committed to. Moreover, it is one I am confident that I will be good at."

Why do you want to work for us?

Make an impact

To make the greatest impact, begin with a personal story, but close with a demonstration of your knowledge and fit for the company. This will make you stand out as an informed and enthusiastic individual who has something more to offer.

"My first experience with ABC Company was two years ago ... The service was so immaculate and welcoming, that I was instantly impressed. Following this experience I became a frequent customer and, when I decided to apply for this position, I was in no doubt who I want to work for.

Once I started to research the company further, I was pleased to discover that the company's corporate culture holds true with my own values and beliefs. Specifically the open door policy and customer comfort initiatives. This discovery reinforced my desire further and confirmed my belief that I will indeed complement your existing team."

Why should we hire you?

"As you can see from my résumé, I have worked in client facing roles for the past eight years. So, I am certainly qualified to perform the diverse requirements of this role. Also, the fact that I have been promoted through the ranks is a clear testament to my abilities and the confidence my manager had in me.

More significantly, my character is tailored to the role. As you will have observed during the group assessments, I am a very welcoming and social individual who interacts well with others. I readily adapt to new people and environments, I am hard working and think fast on my feet.

I am confident that these aspects of my personality and experience will enable me to perform the job to the same high standard that exists currently."

Why did you leave your last job?

» No opportunities
"While I enjoyed working for my previous employer, and appreciate the skills I developed while I was there, I felt I was not being challenged enough in the job. After working my way up through the company, there were no further opportunities for advancement."

» Redundancy
"I survived the first layoffs, but unfortunately this one got me."

» Temporary position
"The job was only a temporary position which I took to broaden my experience."

Why were you fired?

» Incompatibility
"I was desperate for work and took the job without fully understanding the expectations. It turned out that my competencies were not a right match for the employer's needs so we agreed that it was time for me to move on to a position that would be more suitable. I certainly learnt a great deal from this experience, and it's not a mistake I will ever repeat."

» Personal reasons
"I had been going through a rough patch in my personal life which, unfortunately, upset my work life. It is regrettable and my circumstances have now changed, but I really wasn't in the position to avoid it at the time"

Sell Yourself

This is the time to shine, so don't be modest. Consider the experience and character traits that are most relevant and transferable to the position and, for greater impact, explain how you have demonstrated these in the past.

Fired?

If you were dismissed from any position, you need to be honest and say so. However, you should be tactful in your answer and turn it into a positive learning experience.

Never:
» Badmouth previous employers, colleagues or bosses.
» Place blame
» Tell lies
» Reveal team incompatibility

Why have you had so many jobs?

» Broaden experience
"I wanted to experience different jobs to broaden my knowledge, skills and experience. This has provided me with a very valuable and rounded skill set."

» Temporary positions
"Due to the lack of full time opportunities in my area, I was only able to secure short term contracts."

» Youth
In my youth, I was unsure about the direction I wanted to take in my career. I have matured a great deal since those days and am now interested in establishing myself into a long term opportunity.

Why were you unemployed for so long?

Note

It is better to say that you chose to take time off between jobs than it is to give the impression that you were unemployable.

» Soft job market
"Unfortunately, I was made redundant and, due to the lack of opportunities, I wasn't able to secure a position. However, I did use the opportunity to further my knowledge and education which has proved very valuable."

» Study
"I wanted to broaden my knowledge base, so I went back into full time study."

» Travel
"I wanted to experience the world before settling into a long term career. I am now well travelled and ready to commit."

» Youth
"In my youth, I felt confused about the direction I wanted my career to take. I am now much more mature and certain in my desired direction."

» Personal reasons
"Personal circumstances prohibited me from taking gainful employment, however, circumstances have now changed and I am ready to get back to work."

Why did you stay with the same employer for so long?

"I was there for several years, but in a variety of different roles. The opportunities for growth were fantastic so it felt as though I was undergoing frequent changes without actually changing employer. I didn't see the need to move on."

Why have you decided to change professions at this stage of your career?

"This career turnaround hasn't come suddenly. I have always wanted to become a (...) and have been gradually mastering the skills needed to perform its tasks. I have now reached a point in my life where I am prepared to make the career and lifestyle change. I want to take advantage of that opportunity while it is presented to me."

What are your best qualities?

"As you will have observed during the group assessments, I am a very welcoming and social individual who interacts well with others, and readily adapts to new people and environments. In fact, my previous supervisor also picked up on these attributes and often asked me to carry out (...) because she knew I would make the clients feel welcome and relaxed.

I am confident that these aspects of my character will enable me to perform the job to the same high standard that exists currently within the company."

What is your greatest weakness?

"I recognise that my (...) skills are a potential area of improvement, which is why I am actively working on developing this area further through a part time (...) training course. Following completion of this course, I intend to further my abilities by studying (...)."

How have you changed in the last five years?

"I feel like I have matured rather than aged five years. The skills I have acquired and the qualities I have developed have changed me enormously, and I know there are parts of me that are still not being utilised half as effectively as they could be. My customer care and communication skills have definitely been improved, and I have a better ability to use my initiative and think on my feet."

Rate your communication skills on a scale of 1 to 10.

"I would rate myself as an 8. I always give my best, but in doing so I increase my skills. I, therefore, always see room for improvement."

Aren't you overqualified for this position?

"I wouldn't say that I am overqualified, but certainly fully qualified. With more than the minimal experience, I offer immediate returns on your investment. Don't you want a winner with the skill sets and attitudes to do just that?"

Back it up

To give your answer substance, back up your statement with examples of when you have demonstrated these qualities.

Be Unique

Trying to highlight too many positive traits will appear random and over the top. Pick just one or two predominant traits which make you unique.

Weakness or undeveloped skill?

The key to answering questions about weaknesses is to focus your response on those skills you are actively learning or planning to develop. This could be assertiveness or leadership. The point is, it is only a weakness because you haven't yet mastered it, and that is why you are working on developing those skills further.

Importantly, you should avoid volunteering examples which involve key competencies, such as customer care or teamwork.

How would you respond if we told you that you have been unsuccessful on this occasion?

"Naturally, I will be a disappointed if I do not secure this job with you because it is something I really want, I feel ready for it, and I have had plenty to contribute. However, I am not one to give up quickly. I will think about where I went wrong and how I could have done better, and I would then take steps towards strengthening my candidacy."

What would you say if I said your skills and experience were below the requirements of this job?

"I would ask what particular aspects of my skills and experience you felt were lacking and address each one of those areas with examples of where my skills and experiences do match your requirements. I would expect that after this discussion you would be left in no doubt about my ability to do this job."

I'm not sure you are suitable for the position. Convince me.

"I am absolutely suitable. In fact, I am confident that I am perfect for this position.

You are looking for someone who is customer focused. Well, as you can see from my résumé, I have worked in client facing roles for eight years so have had plenty of experience dealing with the various aspects. I also run a successful business that relies on customer satisfaction. The fact that I am still in business, and have a solid and increasing client base, is a clear testament to my abilities.

Furthermore, you need someone who has a calm approach, and retains their composure in the face of adversity. Again, I have demonstrated this capability on several occasions throughout my career.

Beyond this, I have a friendly and optimistic character. I am hard working, I thrive on challenges and will always strive to deliver the highest standard of service to your customers.

I am confident that my skills, experience and personal qualities will complement your existing team and allow me to make a positive contribution to the company's ongoing success."

Why should we hire you for this position rather than another applicant?

"I can't tell you why you should hire me instead of another candidate but, I can tell you why you should hire me."

Caution!

Try not to be thrown off by the implied failure of these questions. The recruiters are simply testing your reaction and want to see what action you would take.

Why should we hire you instead of someone with previous experience?

"Although I might not have (...) experience, I have the necessary skills to make an impressive start, and the willingness to learn and improve. Sometimes, employers do better when they hire people who don't have a great deal of repetitive experience. That way, they can train these employees in their methods and ways of doing the job. Training is much easier than untraining."

Where do you picture yourself in five years?

"I very much hope that I shall be with ABC Company in five years time. By which time, I will have made a significant contribution to the company, will have become an experienced senior member of the team, and will be working on new ways to advance my career further."

If offered the job, how long will you stay with us?

"I'm approaching this job with a long term view. I hope to make enough of a contribution the company that I can move up through the ranks to become an experienced senior member of the team."

Can we contact previous employers for references?

"Yes, absolutely. I'm confident that all my references will be favourable and will confirm what we've discussed here today."

Do you think the customer is always right?

"Whilst every customer is important, they are certainly not always right. Those who exhibit abusive behaviour, or do anything to compromise safety are straying beyond the boundary."

How would you define good customer service?

"Good customer service is about constantly and consistently meeting customer's expectations by providing a friendly, efficient and reliable service throughout the life of the service and/or product.

Excellent customer service is about exceeding customer's expectations by going beyond the call of duty. I believe that because no two customers are the same, they deserve to receive a service that is tailored to their individual needs. This is where a service moves beyond being just a satisfactory one, and becomes an excellent one."

What do you think constitutes poor customer service?

"Poor service is when customers are treated with disrespect and provided with a poor quality product and/or service by rude, ignorant and unhelpful staff."

When have you witnessed good customer service?

"I remember when I visited a local restaurant for a luncheon. It had just turned 3pm on a Wednesday afternoon and, much to mine and the management's surprise, they were exceptionally busy with only three waiting staff on duty. Despite the overwhelming rush our waitress, Claire, was very polite and helpful. The staff showed great teamwork as they managed to pull together and deliver an outstanding service."

When have you witnessed poor customer service?

"I needed a particular material for a dress I was making. In most stores the salesperson would give me a quick 'no' before I finished explaining what I was looking for. I hadn't really noticed until I experienced the opposite service in another smaller fabric store."

What do you enjoy about providing customer care?

"The most enjoyable aspect I would have to say is that because I genuinely care about my client's satisfaction, it rewards me personally when I know that they are happy with the job I did. This, in turn, drives me to do better."

What do you dislike about providing customer care?

"Providing good customer care can be a challenge, and some people may view that negatively, but I view each challenge as an opportunity to develop and grow. So, because I am committed to developing myself, I welcome and enjoy the challenges of providing customer care. It is something I have become very good at."

What do you find most challenging about providing customer service?

"Providing customer service is a challenge in itself. Because people are unpredictable by their very nature, you have to always expect the unexpected and be prepared to go beyond the call of duty and deal with issues as they arrive."

How would you deal with a customer who is not right but believes he is right?

"I would explain the company's rules and policies to the customer in a calm, professional and positive manner. Hopefully, this should clarify any misconceptions that the customer may have."

Do you prefer to work alone or as part of a team?

"I am happy either way, and equally efficient at both. So, whether I prefer to work alone or in a team would depend on the best way to complete the job.

I do, however, have a preference towards team spirit. As well as the interaction, there is greater satisfaction when you share the joy of completing a task."

Are you a team player?

"Absolutely I am. As you will have observed during the group assessments, I interact well with others, and readily adapt to new people. I am a good listener, I respect other people's opinions and I can be relied on to contribute to the overall goal.

In fact, my previous supervisor used to say that my infectious optimism created excitement in other team members and resulted in a greater team effort and higher output."

Do you work well under pressure?

"Absolutely. Because pressure is the result of a new challenge, I perceive pressure as an opportunity to develop and grow. The more challenges I experience, the better my skills become, and the less I feel the pressure of subsequent challenges. So, because I am committed to developing myself, I welcome the challenges of pressure."

How often do you lose your temper?

"I never lose my temper. I regard that sort of behaviour as counterproductive and inappropriate. By losing your temper, you cannot possibly resolve a problem. Even if you're completely right, losing your temper often destroys your ability to convince others of this."

What makes you angry or impatient?

"Anger to me means loss of control, and I'm not the kind of person who loses control. It is counterproductive and inappropriate, and doesn't gain anything of value.

When I feel stress building up, instead of getting angry or impatient, I take a deep breath and begin to focus on the positives."

Interviewing the Interviewer

This portion of the interview is a real chance for you to shine and set yourself apart from all the other candidates. Therefore, it is a good idea to prepare one or two intelligent questions in advance.

The questions you ask, and how you ask them, say a lot about you, your motives, your depth of knowledge about the company and the position itself.

Guidelines

The questions you ask should follow these guidelines:

» Don't ask questions that could be easily answered through your own research.

» Ask questions which demonstrate a genuine interest in and knowledge of the company and the position.

» Demonstrate that you know just that little bit more than is required.

Question About Suitability

Asking recruiters to raise their concerns about your suitability will provide you with an opportunity to follow up and reassure the recruiter.

» Do you have any reservations about my ability to do this job?

» What do you foresee as possible obstacles or problems I might have?

» Is there anything else I need to do to maximise my chances of getting this job?

» How does my background compare with others you have interviewed?

» Is there anything else you'd like to know?

» What do you think are my strongest assets and possible weaknesses?

» Do you have any concerns that I need to clear up in order to be a considered candidate?

Questions About the Recruiter

Asking recruiters about their views and experience in the job or working with the company will demonstrate your genuine interest and motives.

- » How did you find the transition in relocating to ...?
- » Why did you choose to work at (...)?
- » What is it about this company that keeps you working here?
- » It sounds as if you really enjoy working here, what have you enjoyed most about working for (...)?

General Questions

- » How would you describe the company culture?
- » I feel my background and experience are a good fit for this position, and I am very interested. What is the next step?
- » Yes, when do I start?

No Questions

- » I did have plenty of questions, but we've covered them all during our discussions. I was particularly interested in ... but we've dealt with that thoroughly.
- » I had many questions, but you've answered them all you have been so helpful. I'm even more excited about this opportunity than when I applied.

Questions to Avoid

You should avoid asking questions such as those following as they will make you appear selfishly motivated.

- » How many day's holiday allowances will I receive?
- » What is the salary?
- » When will I receive a pay increase?
- » Are there any staff or family discounts?

Journal Notes

Part 4

Conclude

Follow Up
You're Hired

Follow Up

Sending a Thank You Letter

Writing a follow up letter to express appreciation and thanks for the interview demonstrates good business etiquette and also presents an opportunity to make one final positive impression before hiring decisions are made.

To make the most of this opportunity, it is important to cover the following key points:

» Show appreciation and thanks for the company's interest in you

» Reiterate you interest in the position and company

» Follow up with any additional requested information

» Address unresolved points

» Remind of your suitability for the role

Note:

If you met with more than one recruiter, consider extending the courtesy by sending them all thank you letters.

Guidelines

» Letter or email
While emails are more convenient to send, they also risk being perceived as less personal. Traditional letters, on the other hand, are much more formal and yet they also give a personal touch. So, unless online channels have been the primary means of communication or a preference toward email has been specifically implied, I would suggest sending a traditional letter in standard business format.

Retain Consistency

To retain consistency, your thank you letter should continue the theme and format used for your cover letter (See page 73). When viewed as an entire package, it will create a very professional and consistent image.

» Typed or handwritten
Handwritten letters are very personal and should be reserved for short notes. A typed letter in standard business format will work well for a formal thank you letter.

Timing

Plan to send out thank you letters within 24 hours following the interview. Emails can be sent that same evening so that it is in their inbox the following morning.

» Express your enthusiasm
Be sure that the tone of the letter conveys your interest and enthusiasm for both the job and the company. Reiterate your suitability and summarise your strong points as they relate to the job, but don't oversell yourself as you may appear desperate. Keep the letter focused and to the point.

Proofread

Make sure you convey a professional image by being certain that it reads well, and is free from spelling mistakes and grammatical errors. If possible, have a trusted friend proofread it before you send it out.

» Address unresolved points
If necessary, you could use the opportunity to address any issues or questions that came up during the interview that you feel you did not fully answer. However, don't draw unnecessary attention to anything which may be perceived as negative and never apologise. Maintain a positive, confident tone.

16 Any Road • Any Where
Any Town • AN8 9SE
United Kingdom
+44 (0)4587 875848 • Jane.Doe@Anymail.com

Attn: Ms Loren   25 February 2011
ABC Company
London
SW9 0DD
UNITED KINGDOM

Dear Ms Loren

Thank you very much for providing time from your busy schedule to talk with me about the (postion) opening at ABC Company. I truly appreciate your time and consideration in interviewing me.

I felt a wonderful rapport not only with you, but with all the team members I met with. I am further convinced that I will compliment your team and make a positive contribution to the company's ongoing success.

As you requested, I have enclosed a list of references whom you may contact to further confirm my prior work accomplishments.

I am very interested in working for you and look forward to hearing from you once the final decisions are made. Please feel free to contact me if you need any further information.

Thank you for your time and consideration.

Yours sincerely,

Jane Doe
Encl

Figure 16.   Thank You Letter Sample

What Happens Next?

Following the final interview, company's aim to follow up with candidates within two to six weeks. Those who are successful will receive a job offer by email, telephone and/or letter within this time frame, while those who have been unsuccessful will usually receive a computer generated letter.

In the instance that no contact has been made within the timescale noted, it is typically because the company is no longer considering the candidates application.

For those candidates who have been successful, you will be advised of the various pre joining clearance requirements. These may include:

- » Criminal records check
- » Reference checks
- » Joining forms

Once the required steps of the process have been completed, the company will make the necessary arrangements to deliver the employment contract and relevant documentation. You will also be given final clearance to resign from your current employer.

Coping with Setbacks

It may seem counter intuitive to provide coping strategies for rejection in an interview guidance book, however, in an unstable economy such as we are experiencing today, rejection is an unfortunate outcome that some candidates will ultimately face.

So, rather than be crushed by this outcome, I have put together the following tips for coping with, learning from and moving forward following a setback.

Prepare
The popular saying 'Prepare for the worst, but hope for the best' certainly applies in interview scenarios. If we attend the interview with an open mind, our attitude will be more relaxed, we will be better prepared and our coping abilities will be greatly enhanced.

Assess
Faced with rejection, it can be easy to misplace blame on ourselves, others or on the general circumstances. But, if we are to learn and grow from our experience, we must be objective and logical in our assessment rather than making rash and unsubstantiated assumptions.

Note

In some cases, employment contracts are dispatched to candidates prior to the clearances being given. In this instance, do not resign from your current employment until you are formally advised to do so by the recruitment team.

A rejection is nothing more than a necessary step in the pursuit of success.

Bo Bennett

Firstly, we need to reflect on our own performance to establish any possible areas for improvement. We can then make adjustments as necessary and shift our focus to the next opportunity.

Firstly, we need to reflect on our own performance to establish any possible areas for improvement. In this assessment, we could ask:

- » Did I dress appropriately?
- » How did I sound?
- » Did I arrive on time?
- » Did I remember to smile?
- » Did I appear confident and relaxed?
- » Could my answers have been improved?
- » Did I maintain appropriate eye contact?
- » Did I establish rapport with the recruiter?

If this assessment identifies any weaknesses, we can make adjustments as necessary and shift our focus to the next opportunity.

Accept
Sometimes factors exist that are beyond our control and the unfortunate outcome may not have been directly influenced by our performance at all. In this instance, all we can do is accept the outcome and shift our focus to the next opportunity.

Be Positive
Whatever the reason for rejection, it is important to treat each setback as a learning experience. So, don't become obsessive or overly critical, keep an open mind and be open to change if necessary. By handling the setback in this way, we will move forward and succeed much more quickly.

Be Objective
When assessing your performance, avoid being overly and unnecessarily critical. In order to gain the most benefit from this learning experience, it is important to remain objective.

> There are no failures - just experiences and your reactions to them.
>
> Tom Krause

You're Hired

So you've survived the assessment process and now you're hearing those magic words 'you're hired', congratulations. This is an exciting moment and you should be very proud of your achievement. Now indulge in the moment, share the excitement and engage in celebration with your family and friends before returning here to learn what happens next.

Conditional Offer

The initial offer of employment is often subject to candidates meeting certain conditions and preemployment checks, such as:

» Satisfactory references

» Criminal record check

» Signed contract of employment

» Presentation of original academic and professional qualifications

If any of the conditions are not met, the offer of employment can be withdrawn. For this reason, it is important to hold back from handing in your notice to your current employer until you have met the conditions and a formal contract exists between you and the company. A formal contract exists once you have accepted an unconditional offer and signed contracts have been exchanged.

Background Checks

Prior to commencing employment, the company may conduct background checks, including:

References
Typically, the contact information for two professional references will be required. However, in some instances, company's may request details extending as far back as five years.

Common referee questions include:

» Please confirm starting and ending employment dates for (...) at your company

» Why did (...) leave the company?

» What position did (...) hold?

» Please describe the job responsibilities

- » Please describe (...) attendance level
- » Please describe (...) biggest accomplishment while working within the company
- » Please describe (...) strong and weak points
- » Would you rehire (...) if the opportunity was presented?
- » Do you feel (...) would be a good fit for this position of (...)?
- » Is there anything I haven't asked that you would like to share?

When selecting potential referees, ensure you select those people who can attest to your capabilities, such as managers, supervisors or team leaders. Where these are unavailable second choices could include colleagues, customers and academic professors.

Criminal Record Check
Depending on the nature of the position, a valid Criminal Record Check (CRC) may be requested prior to the commencement of employment.

The CRC will include details of:

- » Previous criminal convictions
- » Reprimands
- » Cautions
- » Warnings

If you have any unspent convictions, these will be included on the certificate

Pre-Brief

After you secure permission of your referees, provide him or her with a copy of your résumé. This will ensure a better match of information when the reference is written.

Verify

Verify the contact information of your referees before handing them on to the company. Check the address, phone number and email address, along with the spelling of names and job titles.

Permission

Before you assume a past or current employer will serve as your reference, it is important to secure his or her permission in advance.

Note

Responsibility for obtaining a CRC is the responsibility of the candidate, as are the costs associated with its accrual.

Journal Notes

CPSIA information can be obtained
at www.ICGtesting.com
Printed in the USA
LVHW101513291021
701929LV00019B/2162